Notable Quotables

Notable Quotables
From Women to Women

Compiled by Elaine Cannon

Bookcraft
Salt Lake City, Utah

Library of Congress Catalog Card Number: 92-70188
ISBN 0-88494-822-6

First Printing, 1992

Printed in the United States of America

Wisdom, humor, inspiration and pleasure
for your teachings and your talkings,
your counseling and your comfort,
your givings and your own delight.
The last word on almost everything
a woman cares about.

Contents

Preface

Women know a lot of things they didn't learn in school. Call it woman's intuition, call it sixth sense; call it inspiration from God to his special nurturers of mankind—but women have vast practical knowledge.

Women may have learned what they know at mother's knee, or from minding everybody else's business, or from frankly turning to heaven at every turn, or from doggedly and with delight doing their own thing. One thing is certain: moving through life as an anonymous angel, a slave laborer, a keeper of the flame, women learn a lot about life. It's simply the nature of Eve.

Women listen to other women. Women talk faster, are more creative in problem solving, and quicker in their judgment than any friend, husband, or employer would think possible.

Women work longer hours—the "woman's work is never done" syndrome. The task scene may change from marketplace to fireplace, but they still put in selfless hours upon hours. And they learn as they go.

Women have ultimate concern and belief born of just such experience. And she is always *thinking!*

Women think in adages and quotes. Women are good at spinning a phrase, capsulizing a perspective. They are wakeful, walking dispensers of aphorisms and wisdom to change lives and shorten the time of the one-on-one lecture.

Women aren't mentioned much in history or scripture, but never underestimate the power of a woman behind whatever throne. Every Esther has her day to seize the moment and express an opinion.

Women may not have equal time at the pulpit but they *know* God. Whatever else they do, theirs is the business of being partner with God in caring for his children of all ages and in nudging them into goodness.

All of these attributes make women's opinions absolutely golden!

In *Notable Quotables* you'll find great wisdom on deep and sacred topics. You'll laugh some. You'll bask in lively ideas, brightly spoken opinions, practical helps, nostalgic musings on all sorts of things that women care about.

The quotes come from women across the dispensations of time without regard to cultural background, religious persuasion, race, age, life-style, or daily demands. Whatever their "sun," whatever they are up to, these women have discovered something about life that is charming, true, or helpful at the moment.

Women included in this collection are here because of what they said, not what they are—or were. Truth is where we find it. Truth is truth. Wisdom is wisdom and stands the test of time. And a real woman leaps unabashedly at some new twist to truth.

We crave light and truth and warmth and practical help for our grueling part in things. We yearn for refreshment that is not sodden or shallow. In this collection of thoughts there *is* refreshment for the soul just in the reading of someone else's point of view. Especially when it's from a woman!

Words once spoken are like the proverbial feathers in a breeze. Oh, the things I have heard in a windstorm—or a dinner party. Some aren't printable, of course, but some are so lovely as to mellow the mind—"words that weep and tears that speak." It has been my custom since my earliest days to write down or snip and paste a particularly good quote or idea of worth expressed in a concise form that has crossed my heart and hearing. Sources cannot always be traced now. But to the best of my knowledge and belief, I have given due credit for these notable quotables by women. It is Mr. Emerson and his mousetrap, after all. Whoever said what, and however the words were chosen and arranged, this is a collection of notable quotables by women.

When I was an avid young writer an editor gave me a copy of a famous quotation with which I agree. It goes like this: "I believe that imagination is stronger than knowledge. That myth is more potent than history. That dreams are more powerful than facts. That hope always triumphs over experience. That laughter is the only cure for grief. And I believe that love is stronger than death." All of which women know! I would add that a woman's point of view ought to be listened to. Hence, *Notable Quotables*—women to women.

The quotes are out of context. Take them at face value. They have been overheard, observed, shared, remembered, read, and researched. Credit may have been given where it wasn't due. We may have mixed our authors as well as our metaphors. But there is good stuff here.

Glorious Womanhood

There are two important days in a woman's life—the day she is born and the day she finds out why.

—*Elaine Cannon*

I believe in women. I desire . . . to do those things that would advance women in moral and spiritual, as well as educational work.

—*Emmeline B. Wells*

---

*B*ehold the handmaid of the Lord; be it unto me according to thy word.

—*Mary, mother of Jesus*

---

*I*t is the duty of each one of us to be a holy woman. We shall have elevated aims, if we are holy women.

—*Eliza R. Snow*

*O*ne certainty is that the Lord expects women to have a voice, to speak up, to stand as witnesses of the Lord Jesus Christ.

—*Clare Hardy Johnson*

*B*ecause women take time out for childbearing, they have less tenure than men in their jobs, which translates into lower earnings.

—*Barbara Riskin*

*T*enure? Women want tenure in their jobs like men? What is motherhood but tenure!

—*Christine Cannon*

The serpent beguiled me, and I did eat.

—*Eve*

*W*omen should be as courageous as Eve.

—*Jessie Evans Smith*

*A*fter giving water to Isaac's servant, Rebekah said: "I will draw water for thy camels also, until they have done drinking."

—*Rebekah*

*B*ehold, let thine handmaid be a servant to wash the feet of the servants of my lord.

—*Abigail*

*T*he feeling has been expressed in some circles that marriage is the only measure of worth for women. This is not true. Whether a woman is married or single, the true worth of her life is measured by the ways she has blessed the lives of others.

—*Phyllis Roundy*

I feel strongly that women need to have the kind of education that allows them a number of options. . . . Knowing that I have my [law] degree enhances my sense of self-worth, which is something we all need.

—*Lisa Ramsey Adams*

I was blessed to get an education available to few black women in Africa at that time. Every woman should be able to get an education so she can serve others.

—*Julia Mavimbela*

I like the story of the newlywed who served ham for her first Sunday dinner. The husband noticed the ends of the ham had been cut off and he asked why. "That's the way my mother always did it," the bride replied with a shrug. He asked his wife's mother the same question and got the same answer, "That's the way my mother did it." Finally he asked the grandma, who replied, "That's the only way I could get it into the pan."

—*Winnifred C. Jardine*

*T*here are two things that women do to feel better—two quick fixes: a new hair color and eating. A massage would be better.

—*Sinikka Lasater*

I like to sing driving the car pool. My favorite song is "Take Me Out to the Convent." Second is "I Hope They Call Me on a Mission."

—*Beverly Kisk*

*A*bove all, challenge yourself. You may well surprise yourself at what strengths you have, what you can accomplish.

—Cecile M. Springer

I am a firm believer in the glorious system of priesthood and womanhood.

—Ruth H. Funk

*S*he rose to his requirement, dropped
The playthings of her life
To take the honorable work
Of woman and of wife.

—Emily Dickinson

*A*dvice on campaign behavior for first ladies: Always be on time. Do as little talking as humanly possible. Remember to lean back in the parade so everybody can see the president. Be sure not to get too fat, because you'll have to sit three in the back.

—*Eleanor Roosevelt*

*O*ur life is a faint tracing on the surface of mystery.

—*Annie Dillard*

I have made a plan for my life, as I am in my teens, and no more a child. I am old for my age and don't care much for girls' things. People think I'm wild and queer; but mother understands and helps me. I have not told anyone about my plans but I am going to be good. . . . Now I'm going to *work really*, for I feel a desire to improve and be a help and comfort, not a care and sorrow to my dear mother.

—*Louisa May Alcott*

*I*n Mary Webb's *Precious Bane* . . . what is finally evolved in us is more than the fairy-tale longing that our inner beauty will be seen so clearly it will make us beautiful before the world; it is the longing to be known and loved for all our blemishes, our warts and wens and contradictions, to be "let in" whole.

—*Erika Duncan*

*Y*ou are daughters of God. If each one of you could only have a sure knowledge of this for yourself, you would have a sweet peace in your heart and confidence to meet any challenges life may bring.

—*Jayne B. Malin*

*H*ow odd that girl's life looks
Behind this soft eclipse!
I think that earth seems so
To those in heaven now.

This being comfort, then
That other kind was pain;
But why compare?
I'm wife! stop there!

—*Emily Dickinson*

*W*hich is the woman, which the child?
The joyous laugh that opens doors, steals sugared moments from
    the shelf?
Or the dreamer mixing metaphors with tears to make a book of self
To read aloud in winter's rooms
When summer's sounds have ceased to bloom?

                                      —Katie Louchheim

*B*eing an old maid is like death by drowning—a really delightful
sensation after you have ceased struggling.

                                      —Edna Ferber

*A*t work you worry over the family at home. At home you fret
over work left undone. Behold the working woman's stress.

                                      —Elaine Cannon

Our focus reflects our love and admiration for you. . . . We want you to live lives of spiritual maturity and fulfillment, free of unrealistic comparisons.

—*Elaine L. Jack*

I don't think any change in the world has been more significant than the change in the status of women. . . . A woman's world was her home, her family, and perhaps a little community service. Today a woman's world is as broad as the universe.

—*Belle S. Spafford*

The skin is our body's envelope, the wrapping that delivers us to the world. If we understand how the skin functions in mid-life and adjust our goals and life-styles appropriately, we'll be surprised how much better we can look.

—*Jane Fonda*

*I*f "Rights" are right when they are rightly gained,
"Rights" must be wrong when wrongfully obtained.
The putting forth a hand to take the prize,
Before we fairly win it, is unwise.

—*Eliza R. Snow*

*E*very woman should eat for the long run so she can manage the short stops of crisis.

—*Jane Fonda*

*W*hen five former first ladies and Barbara Bush walked across the courtyard of the Ronald Reagan Presidential Library . . . someone watching interrupted the hush and whispered, "There are the real heroes."

—*Onlooker*

*F*or women, talk is the glue that holds relationships together; it creates connections between people and a sense of community. For men, activities hold relationships together; talk is used to negotiate their position in a group and preserve independence.

—*Deborah Farmer*

*D*on't shut yourself up in a band box because you are a woman, but understand what is going on, and educate yourself to take part in the world's work, for it all affects you and yours.

—*Louisa May Alcott*

*N*one but mothers know each other's feelings when we give up our daughters whom we love and cherish so tenderly to the mercies of a man, and perhaps even a stranger.

—*Emmeline B. Wells*

*P*resented memorial to [Constitutional Convention] committee on sufferage. Was very courteously treated. We all felt it a great day in the history of Utah. The committee informed us they had passed on W[oman] S[uffrage] being ten to five in favor.

—*Ruth May Fox*

*N*ever forget that you have the spark of the divine in you. Whatever you do or don't do won't change this fact.

—*Elaine Cannon*

*B*e true. Be beautiful. Be free. In the midst of segregation and racism Mamma raised us to be independent and free. We saw ourselves as citizens of the world, not of a block.

—*Debbie Allen*

*E*ach girl is special—one of a kind—a child of God, and each must be taught to live his commandments in order to inherit his eternal blessings.

—*Martha H. Tingey*

*H*ave Faith

Seek Knowledge

Safeguard Health

Honor Womanhood

Understand Beauty

Value Work

Love Truth

Taste the Sweetness of Service

Feel Joy

—*"The Spirit of the Hive" (Beehive girls' theme)*

*L*ove of Amusement of our girls is as natural as roses to bloom in June. Make an educator of the ball-room, the Theater, the excursion, combining fun and profit, thus elevating taste and morals while faces are bright, lips gay, and hearts happy.

—*Susa Young Gates*

*M*others, look after your daughters, keep them near you, keep their confidence—that they may be true and faithful.

—*Elmina S. Taylor*

*S*ome women go through life turning on lamps in the evening. Others are themselves a light.

—*Helen Perkes*

A woman can learn a lot from holding a new baby. It is life beginning again—sweet possibilities! No problem in the world is big enough to be remembered.

—*Susan McOmber*

*O*ur girls have need of such an example of graciousness, elegance, refinement, and spirituality.

—*Maria Dougall*

*W*e can have unity in diversity and diversity in unity. We don't have to be like one another to enjoy sisterhood.

—*Barbara W. Winder*

*K*eep pace with the times. . . . Find new and surprising ways to teach girls how to develop every gift and grace of true womanhood.

—*Elmina S. Taylor*

*W*e—believing in the sacred scriptures, and as St. Paul says: "If a woman have long hair, it is a glory to her: for her hair is given her for a covering"—will not hereafter have our heads shorn of their glory.

—Twentieth Ward Women's Retrenchment Association

*T*his is a wonderful world for women. The richness, the hope, the promise of life today, particularly for women, are exciting beyond belief. Nonetheless, we need stout hearts and strong characters; we need knowledge and training; we need organized effort to meet the future.

—Belle S. Spafford

A woman's mind is not an instrument apart from her other being. She does not separate herself as man does, now flesh, now mind, now heart. She is there as one, a unity complete and unified.

—Pearl S. Buck

*T*imes have changed. Elmina Taylor, her six counselors, one secretary, and several "aids" traveled throughout the Territory of Deseret in spring on lumber wagons. Our presidency, two secretaries, and sixty-eight board members traveled throughout the world in jet planes in fewer hours than it took Elmina to travel from Salt Lake to St. George, Utah. Times have changed, the program for girls has changed, but the original purposes and principles have never changed.

—Florence S. Jacobsen

*W*omen need solitude in order to find again the true essence of themselves.

—Anne Morrow Lindbergh

*Y*ou're it, honey. Go for it.

—Anne Wilson Schael

*P*lum brandy . . . years have passed since I bought a bottle, let alone tasted it, perhaps because it belongs to a room that is no longer mine and to a person who is no longer myself.

—*Mary Cantwell*

*W*hat this misguided world, generation needs is a massive group of courageous and caring, wise and unwearying women.

—*Elaine Cannon*

*T*he tragedy of Sarah's early life was that she was barren, but the miracle of her life was that she gave birth to Isaac, Son of Promise, when humanly speaking, the time had passed when she could become a mother.

—*Edith Drew*

*S*hall I go and call to thee a nurse of the Hebrew women, that she may nurse the child for thee?

—*Miriam*

*T*he queen of Sheba . . . lives on now, nearly thirty centuries since her visit [to Solomon in Israel], as a woman whose spirit of adventure and whose resourcefulness, courage, and curiosity have not been surpassed by any queen in history. And certainly her sense of good public and international relations is unparalleled among women of the Bible.

—*Edith Deen*

*T*here are so many options, so much to do, so many demands on women. There is no point in taking one hour to do a ten-minute task, nor should we slap together an hour-worthy project in ten minutes.

—*Elaine Cannon*

*T*he lives of the women of the Bible made patterns of light or of darkness. . . . Watch for the phrase in Kings and Chronicles, "And his mother was . . ." This is usually followed by the phrase, "And he did that which was good in the sight of the Lord," or "And he did that which was evil in the sight of the Lord." In placing the name of the king's mother and the evaluation of his reign side by side, the Hebrews showed how powerful they regarded the role of a mother.

—Edith Deen

*T*he equilibrium that each mother-daughter pair finds will be as different as their personalities. Some will never be comfortable as buddies, no matter how much they respect each other.

—Jennifer Kaylin

*G*ender matters less to women than the causes women espouse.

—Priscilla Painton

*T*here is a special kind of girl who goes where the action is, but only if the action is the right kind. . . . Who centers the happy storm about her, but doesn't stir up one. Who makes a mere event a happening. Who isn't content with contentment. Who doesn't fight the inevitable nor ignore opportunities—but who joins forces with time and fate and rises to every occasion. This special kind of girl knows that the way she moves, the way she speaks, the fragrance about her, and the good things she does mark the difference between herself and the girl who just doesn't really care enough about being a girl. This special kind of girl makes up her own mind after careful, prayerful thought. She sets her own image. She's tasteful, individual, exciting. She's worthwhile and a breath of sweet life.

—Elaine Cannon

*B*lessed art thou among women, and blessed is the fruit of thy womb.

—Elisabeth

I didn't think that having a baby after I'd turned forty was so bad— only that I had to hold her at arm's length to look at her.

—Margie Haynes

*E*va stood looking at Topsy.

There stood the two children, representatives of the two extremes of society. The fair, high-bred child, with her golden head, her deep eyes, her spiritual, noble brow . . . ; and her black, keen, subtle, cringing, yet acute neighbor. There stood the representatives of their races. The Saxon, born of ages of cultivation, command, education, physical and moral eminence; the Afric, born of ages of oppression, submission, ignorance, toil and vice!

. . . When Miss Ophelia expatiated on Topsy's naughty, wicked conduct, the child looked perplexed and sorrowful, but said, sweetly,

"Poor Topsy, why need you steal? You're going to be taken good care of, now. I'm sure I'd rather give you anything of mine, than have you steal it."

It was the first word of kindness the child had ever heard in her life; and the sweet tone and manner struck strangely on the wild, rude heart, and a sparkle of something like a tear shone in the keen, round, glittering eye; but it was followed by the short laugh. . . . No! the ear that has never heard anything but abuse is strangely incredulous of anything so heavenly as kindness; and Topsy only thought Eva's speech something funny and inexplicable,—she did not believe it.

—*Harriet Beecher Stowe*

*D*o you expect to marry?" teased Mrs. Pinkhurst.

"In the dim, distant future, maybe; but that's on the lap of the Gods . . . meanwhile, whether or not, I intend to take up some work and succeed at it!"

—*Ida Stewart Peay*

*T*he Lord knows us for what we are, and eventually, everyone else does, too.

—*Lorraine Henriod*

*N*othing in my life, not even a concert career, can surpass in importance the divine calling of being a mother.

—*Sally Peterson Brinton*

God

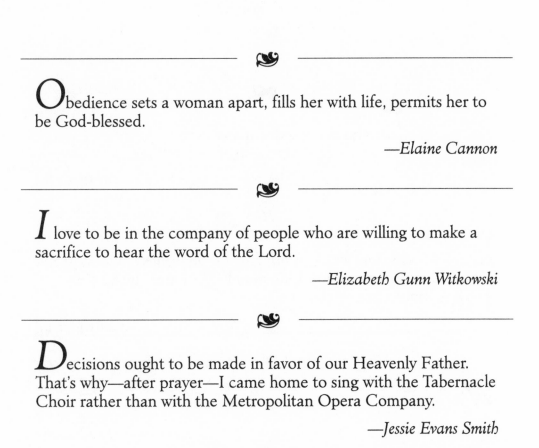

Obedience sets a woman apart, fills her with life, permits her to be God-blessed.

—*Elaine Cannon*

I love to be in the company of people who are willing to make a sacrifice to hear the word of the Lord.

—*Elizabeth Gunn Witkowski*

Decisions ought to be made in favor of our Heavenly Father. That's why—after prayer—I came home to sing with the Tabernacle Choir rather than with the Metropolitan Opera Company.

—*Jessie Evans Smith*

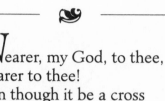

*N*earer, my God, to thee,
Nearer to thee!
E'en though it be a cross
That raiseth me.
Still all my song shall be
Nearer, my God, to thee!

—*Sarah Flower Adams*

*E*arth's crammed with heaven,
And every common bush afire with God.

—*Elizabeth Barrett Browning*

*J*esus is the only one who can bring us to forgiveness. He waits for us to turn our hearts over to him; then he performs the healing, changing, finishing miracles.

—*Holly Metcalf*

*W*hat would Christ do if he were in my situation?

—*Chieko N. Okazaki*

I know my prayers are being heard—and answered. And I can sing with sincerity: Sweet hour of prayer!

—*Winnifred C. Jardine*

*I*f I may but touch his garment, I shall be whole.

—*Diseased woman*

*R*ebellious people are those who either have never heard the gospel of Jesus Christ or have not understood it. Receptive people think the gospel is true—but their actions lag behind. Righteous people *know* Christ and practice what he preached.

—*Elaine Cannon*

*O*ur faith in the present dies out long before our faith in the future.

—*Ruth Benedict*

*I*n the process of working with others you'll experience great growth in yourself, both emotional and spiritual. Your bond with your Heavenly Father will strengthen unmeasurably. This is both a calling and a sacred trust.

—*Betty Pettit*

*I*f we want to be used for the benefit of mankind—helping the Lord with *his* mission—we must ourselves be in a position to be used by him.

—*Elaine Cannon*

*S*atan loves to get us feeling sorry for ourselves.

—*Barbara Barrington Jones*

*I*n what may seem to be the darkest of times, if we will but reach up to our Father (instead of away from him to alternative counterfeits) he will hold our hand through the ordeal.

—*Kathryn S. Smith*

*T*he Lord, creator of life, has given us information to act upon that is guaranteed by him to guide us to our goal of life eternal.

—*Elaine Cannon*

I know there are no errors,
In the great Eternal plan.

—*Ella Wheeler Wilcox*

*I*n sky and land and river wide,
The work of God I see.

—*Matilda Watts Cahoon*

*W*hen faced with a difficult decision or challenge, [ask], "What would the Lord have me do? Would I do it for the Lord?"

—*Bonnie Pinegar*

I am a twelfth-generation descendant of William Bradford, the second governor of the Plymouth colony, and I deeply admire him. He walked with God and that is what I wish to do.

—*Mary Ellen Pogue*

*I*f we had everything we wanted and needed without asking of Heavenly Father, we would lose sight of the hand of God in our lives.

—*Elaine Cannon*

*G*od *does* notice us and watch over us, but it is usually through someone else that he meets our needs.

—*Susan McOmber*

Where, when my aching grows,
Where, when I languish,
Where, in my need to know, where can I run?
Where is the quiet hand to calm my anguish?
Who, who can understand?
He, only One.

—Emma Lou Thayne

We have been promised that "the prayers of the faithful shall be heard." My personal testimony is that this is so.

—Mary Schindler Nielsen

To believe in God is to know all the rules will be fair and there will be wonderful surprises.

—Sister Mary Curita

My testimony has been my anchor and my stay, my satisfaction in times of joy and gladness, my comfort in times of sorrow and discouragement.

—*Amy Brown Lyman*

Seek for a testimony, as you would . . . for a diamond concealed. If someone told you by digging long enough in a certain spot you would find a diamond of unmeasured wealth, do you think you would begrudge time or strength, or means spent to obtain that treasure? Then I will tell you that if you will dig in the depths of your own hearts you will find, with the aid of the Spirit of the Lord, the pearl of great price, the testimony of the truth of this work.

—*Zina D. H. Young*

Now I know of a surety . . . that the Lord hath protected my sons, and delivered them out of the hands of Laban, and given them power whereby they could accomplish the thing which the Lord hath commanded them.

—*Sariah*

*T*here was a time when I was totally bereft and couldn't imagine why I couldn't feel Heavenly Father around me. But looking back I clearly could mark the path he silently carried me.

—*Rebecca Cannon*

*T*o follow truth as blind men long for light,
To do my best from dawn of day till night,
To keep my heart fit for His holy sight,
    And answer when He calls.
      This is my task.

—*Maude Louise Ray*

O help me Father in heaven to overcome and resist temptation in every form or shape.

—*Emmeline B. Wells*

*I*n these distressing times, the spirit of the Lord was with us to comfort and sustain us, and we had a sure testimony that we were being persecuted for the Gospel's sake, and that the Lord was angry with none save those who acknowledge not his hand in all things.

—*Bathsheba W. Smith*

*T*he gospel assures you that your value is not dependent on your looks or material possessions.

—*Elaine L. Jack*

*E*ver since I could understand, the Gospel has meant everything to me. It has been my very breath, my mantle of protection against temptation, my consolation in sorrow, my joy and glory throughout all my days, and my hope of eternal life. "The Kingdom of God or nothing" has been my motto.

—*Ruth May Fox*

*I*t is useless, sisters, for you to attempt the duties of your exalted callings . . . without the constant companionship of the Spirit of God.

—*Susa Young Gates*

*F*irst of all that I would crave as the richest of heaven's blessings would be wisdom from my Heavenly Father bestowed daily.

—*Emma Hale Smith*

I don't always kneel when I pray. My prayers fly heavenward all day long—while I bake or drive or comfort. I mean no disrespect to Heavenly Father, I just need him constantly while the work of woman goes on.

—*Helen Lee Goates*

*U*nless inside, where no one sees, our soul is kneeling, too, a prayer is not so likely to get through.

—*Elaine Cannon*

We go from God to God—so let the space between be filled with beauty, conquering things base and mean.

—*Evelyn H. Healey*

The Christian Sunday should be a festival, gathering up all the life of the week and offering it to God in worship and then spending the day in a way which most truly promotes joy and happiness and refreshment for oneself and for other people.

—*Olive Wyon*

He paints the lily of the field,
Perfumes each lily bell.
If he so loves the little flowers,
I know he loves me well.

—*Maria Straus*

*D*ear Lord, who made the face of me not all that I would have it be, not really homely, only plain, but strong and patient in the main. Yet one, a man apart, who found me fair and gave his heart. Now Lord, that I have grown more sage . . . into middle age. I only ask, as face grows lined of countenance, it be described as kind; that wrinkles by my eyes will show a little humor as I go; that I may view my humble scene with glance of one content, serene, through grateful, shining eyes that see the blessings you have given me.

—Ruth Perry

*D*on Ricardo Evertom, said the priest, has left footprints in this soil that neither rain nor wind can scrap away. Nationality and language do not separate friends. . . . It makes no difference what a man believes if he is a good person.

—Harriet Doerr

*M*y God would never deliberately bring harm to anyone. But if it happens, if it simply happens due to wind and rain and weather and man's own mistakes, then God has promises to keep: Life continuing. An even richer, fuller, brighter ongoing life to compensate.

—Marjorie Holmes

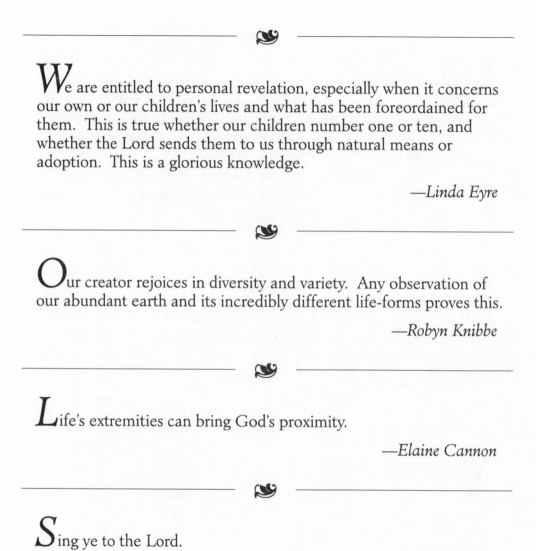

*W*e are entitled to personal revelation, especially when it concerns our own or our children's lives and what has been foreordained for them. This is true whether our children number one or ten, and whether the Lord sends them to us through natural means or adoption. This is a glorious knowledge.

—*Linda Eyre*

*O*ur creator rejoices in diversity and variety. Any observation of our abundant earth and its incredibly different life-forms proves this.

—*Robyn Knibbe*

*L*ife's extremities can bring God's proximity.

—*Elaine Cannon*

*S*ing ye to the Lord.

—*Miriam*

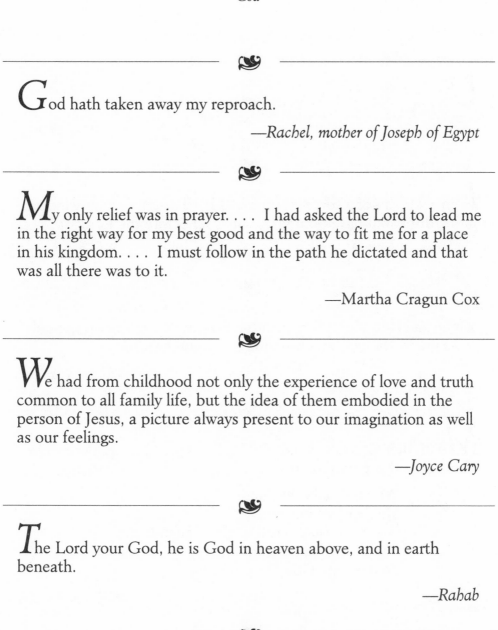

God hath taken away my reproach.

—*Rachel, mother of Joseph of Egypt*

My only relief was in prayer. . . . I had asked the Lord to lead me in the right way for my best good and the way to fit me for a place in his kingdom. . . . I must follow in the path he dictated and that was all there was to it.

—Martha Cragun Cox

We had from childhood not only the experience of love and truth common to all family life, but the idea of them embodied in the person of Jesus, a picture always present to our imagination as well as our feelings.

—*Joyce Cary*

The Lord your God, he is God in heaven above, and in earth beneath.

—*Rahab*

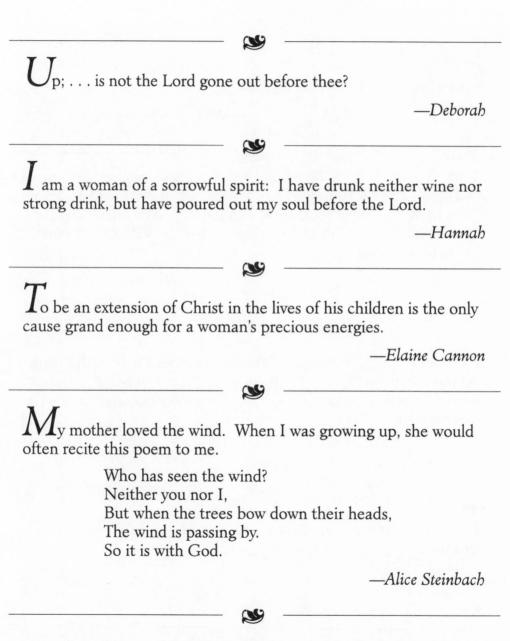

*U*p; . . . is not the Lord gone out before thee?

—*Deborah*

I am a woman of a sorrowful spirit: I have drunk neither wine nor strong drink, but have poured out my soul before the Lord.

—*Hannah*

*T*o be an extension of Christ in the lives of his children is the only cause grand enough for a woman's precious energies.

—*Elaine Cannon*

*M*y mother loved the wind. When I was growing up, she would often recite this poem to me.

> Who has seen the wind?
> Neither you nor I,
> But when the trees bow down their heads,
> The wind is passing by.
> So it is with God.

—*Alice Steinbach*

*H*ow shall this be, seeing I know not a man?

—*Mary, mother of Jesus*

I was reared in a traditional Catholic home. Never once could I question the love my parents and grandparents had for the Lord, as well as for one another. . . . [Now] in living the true gospel of Jesus Christ as a Latter-day Saint, I have complete assurance that God does live and that he hears and answers prayers.

—*Darlene B. Curtis*

*L*ord, dost thou not care that my sister hath left me to serve alone? bid her therefore that she help me.

—*Martha*

I know that Messias cometh, which is called Christ: when he is come, he will tell us all things.

—*Woman of Samaria*

*I*f our testimonies aren't growing they are in danger of becoming weaker.

—*Nona Dyer*

*S*ince my baptism after I graduated from high school, my life has never been happier, never more fulfilled. As I learned to use the Holy Ghost, I was blessed to know how true and how exciting the gospel is.

—*Julie Hanwiller*

*R*emember that the Lord sustains you in your sickness and affliction, in your struggles—not because you are perfect or great but because he is.

—*Elaine Cannon*

*I*t is my strong contention that there is an infinitely higher thrill which, like climbing a mountain or singing a beautiful song, once experienced never stops begging to be repeated. That thrill has its beginnings in the private of personal discovery of revealed truth— the universal laws by which God is governed and by which he governs. It has its development in private and personal decisions to test that law through acts of faith followed by effort. And the consummation of that thrill comes in watching and, indeed, experiencing body and soul the miraculous unfolding of events as they proceed by methods far beyond our feeble capacities to dream of.

—JoAnn Ottley

*B*y strict obedience Jesus won.

—Eliza R. Snow

I'll go where you want me to go, dear Lord . . . ;
I'll say what you want me to say . . . ;
I'll be what you want me to be.

—Mary Brown

*U*pon the cross he meekly died
For all mankind to see
That death unlocks the passageway
Into eternity.

—*Vilate Raile*

*H*e will regard his people's cry, the widow's tear, the orphan's
moan.

—*Eliza R. Snow*

*D*oes faith begin to fail . . . ?
Say not the Father hath not heard your prayer;
You shall have your desire, sometime, somewhere.

—*Ophelia G. Adams*

*T*he Comforter will teach you.

—*Mary Judd Page*

When I'm home or far away,
Heav'nly Father, hear me pray.

—*Mary R. Jack*

I urge you to join me in this resolution: We *will* "stand as witnesses of God at all times and in all things, and in all places"—and at *all* costs.

—*Vivian R. Cline*

*M*ind you, I'm going into the bedroom now to talk things over with Heavenly Father.

—*Martha H. Tingey*

*A*ll over the world at the end of day,
Heav'nly Father's children kneel down and pray. . . .
Our Heavenly Father hears them;
He understands each tongue.
Our Heav'nly Father knows them;
He loves them, loves them, ev'ry one.

—Peggy Hill Ryskamp

*W*hatever our personal burden or cross to bear might be, we are here. We live! We Learn! The Grand Adventure is under way for us. Terrible as our trials might be, we are blessed and not abandoned by God.

—Elaine Cannon

*B*e it unto me according to thy word. . . . My soul doth magnify the Lord.

—Mary

---

*P*ity those who cannot say: Thy will be done not mine, today.

—*Elaine Cannon*

---

*L*ean on thyself until thy strength is tried,
Then ask God's help; it will not be denied.

—*Ella Wheeler Wilcox*

---

*J*ust before bedtime prayers, evaluate each day. Make plans for tomorrow that will move you toward your long-range goal. Strive for a close partnership with God in making your dreams come true.

—*Florence S. Jacobsen*

---

*T*hrough prayer, our free agency is used to admit and confess our deep desire to have God's help in our lives.

—*Elaine Cannon*

---

*T*he gospel of Jesus Christ is the way of life. It assures that if we live by its teachings, our mechanism from within will say to the world, "I'm happy, I'm not afraid."

—*LaRue Longden*

I know the Lord is anxious to respond to us if we will only turn to him.

—*Dwan J. Young*

Gratitude

A life's record with God in the details can be a spiritual feast for our souls. When we count our blessings on paper, our gratitude soars. It is all so evident.

—Elaine Cannon

---

*L*et your hearts rejoice in gladness!

—Mabel Jones Gabbott

---

*T*hank you, God, for the dignity and beauty of self. The precious innate self. The only thing that can't be taken from us. The only thing we really own.

—Marjorie Holmes

---

*S*ee, Lord, my coat hangs in tatters, like homespun old thread? All that I had of yet, all my strength, I have given in hard work and kept nothing back for myself. Now my poor head swings to offer up all the loneliness of my heart. Dear God, still on my thickened legs I stand here before you; your unprofitable servant. Oh! of your goodness, give me gentle death.

—Carmen Birnos De Gasstold

A search of one's life and soul will reveal the hand of God. The outpouring of his blessings come with our afflictions, not in spite of them. Afflictions be praised!

—Elaine Cannon

I can gratefully count dozens of times when my life has been guided, protected, or simply touched by the Holy Ghost.

—Sonja Eddings Brown

*I*n this view of the world, the job of heroes is to enlighten the world by loving it—starting with themselves. Their task is not to slay the dragon—within or without—but to affirm the deepest level of truth about it: that is, that we are all one.

—*Carol Pearson*

I thank God for my handicaps, for through them, I have found myself, my work, and my God.

—*Helen Keller*

*Y*ou must not think that I feel, in spite of it having ended in such defeat, that my "life has been wasted" here, or that I would exchange it with that of anyone I know.

—*Isak Dinesen*

*S*is. M[arkham] and I are nicely seated in an ox wagon, on a chest with a brass kettle and a soap box for our foot stools, thankful that we are so well off.

—*Eliza R. Snow*

A song from the heart will be answered with a blessing on the head. I've been blessed trying to repay my Heavenly Father for his gift to me.

—*Jessie Evans Smith*

*L*ife is school, life is learning. Count your blessings and abide.

—*Elaine Cannon*

*D*on't think of gray in your hair. Think of the fun you had putting it there.

—*Anna Greenwood*

*P*hysically burdened as I am I count each day a bonus and begin it with my exercise in joy—counting my blessings.

—*Louise Lake*

*W*e bow our heads and close our eyes
And say a little prayer.
We thank our Father graciously
For blessings we all share.

—*Anna Johnson*

*T*hanksgiving is my favorite holiday . . . no costumes, no suitcases, no gifts, no basket grass and half-eaten marshmallow eggs, no flags to fly, no pageants to prepare. Just friends and family bowed together before Heavenly Father.

—*Katherine Wirthlin Cannon*

*T*ake a hard look at those things which we needlessly, foolishly turn into burdens when they were meant to be blessings.

—*Elaine Cannon*

*A*t every one of the places we stayed on this journey we had prayers immediately after the dinner-supper, and prayers again before breakfast. No one was excused. . . . The Mormons . . . kneel at once, while the head of the household, or an honored guest prays aloud. . . . They spend very little time in ascriptions, but ask for what they need, and thank Him for what He has given. . . . [They] take it for granted that God knows our familiar names and titles, and will ask a blessing on [a particular individual by name], . . . I liked this when I became used to it.

—*Mrs. Thomas L. Kane*

*W*e're seeing countries all around the world now who are trying to have something like our Bill of Rights to protect them. We don't realize how fortunate we are.

—*Caroline Kennedy*

*F*reedom is man's birthright,
A sacred, living rampart,
A pulse beat of humanity . . .
A throb of a nation's heart!

—*Clara Smith Reber*

*H*appily, I can say that I have never had to compromise my standards to satisfy any demands of public office.

—*Senator Paula Hawkins*

*T*o the past, the present, and the future, I dedicate this book. To the past because I came out of it, to the present because I live in it, to the future because my children shall inherit it.

—*Ruth May Fox*

*C*ount your night by stars, not blackness,
Count your time by good deeds done.

—*Ethel C. Smith*

*H*appiness comes from noticing and enjoying the little things in life. I've counted at least 1,000 things to be happy about.

—*Barbara Ann Kipfer*

*C*ontentment is not the fulfillment of what you want, but the realization of how much you already have.

—*Kiki Knickerbocker*

*M*y work with the human body confirms my belief in God. Our gratitude to the Creator should be fresh and forever.

—*DeLoris Orvin*

*S*ing ye to the Lord, for he hath triumphed gloriously.

—*Miriam, sister of Moses*

*T*hank you Lord, for trying me: I pray my faith will be sufficient to awaken the miracle in me.

—*Marilyn J. Drumright*

*B*ecause I have been given much, I too must give.

—*Grace Noll Crowell*

*B*ack of the loaf is the snowy flour,
And back of the flour, the mill,
And back of the mill is the wheat and the shower,
The sun and the Father's will.

—*Anonymous*

I remember standing under one of the trees in the park area, looking up with delight and wonder at its height, its clean-lined branches, and the leafy pattern against the sky. From the tree came a sense of peace and benediction. There was a sequestered feeling of semi-isolation and privacy. One could live with one's dreams and sense infinity.

—*Ramona Wilcox Cannon*

*V*alue yourself. As a child of God, hold yourself with such reverence that you are protected against Satan's weapons: temptation, depression, jealousy, anger, self-pity, self-righteousness.

—*Elaine Cannon*

*T*hank God for the blessings of the past and for the future so full of promise and wonderful possibilities.

—*Mae T. Nystrom*

Great Homes

*W*hat would we do without children? Well, for starters, nothing!

—*Elaine Cannon*

*I*n the heav'ns are parents single?
No, the thought makes reason stare!
Truth is reason; truth eternal
Tells me I've a mother there.

—*Eliza R. Snow*

What is a home? A roof to keep out the rain. Four walls to keep out the wind. Floors to keep out the cold. Yes, but a home is more than that. It is the laugh of a baby, the song of a mother, the strength of a father. Warmth of loving hearts, light from happy eyes, kindness, loyalty, comradeship. That is home. God bless it.

—*Ernestine Shuman-Heink*

We have to learn to make our heaven before we can live in it.

—*Paula Wescott*

A true family is
not always
one's own flesh
and blood.
It is a climate
of the heart.

—*Shirley Barksdale*

*H*ome is where warm, circling arms go all the way around.

—*Caroline Eyring Miner*

*S*o long as there are homes to which men turn
At close of day;
So long as there are homes where children are,
Where women stay—
If love and loyalty and faith be found
Across those sills—
A stricken nation can recover from
Its gravest ills.

—*Grace Noll Crowell*

*E*vents like the Oakland fire—a horrendous disaster where people lost everything—make you do some fast thinking about what you would take with you if you had only a few minutes to grab something. It cuts right to the quick about what's really important—it isn't the house, it's the home.

—*Susan McOmber*

*I*f I had influence with the good fairy who is supposed to preside over the christening of all children, I should ask that her gift to each child in the world be a sense of wonder so indestructible that it would last throughout life, as an antidote against the boredom and disenchantment of later years, the sterile preoccupation with things that are artificial, the alienation from the sources of our strength.

—*Rachel Carson*

*M*y mother says it's better to give than to receive—that's all right for *her* to say.

—*Tiffany Theuyer*

*W*hen I say to one of my children, "Look, why do you always choose the hard way?" I get the answer, "Mom, why do you always say 'always'?"

—*Janice Moyle*

*T*here is great satisfaction in building a house, but that is nothing compared to the overwhelming joy in building an outpost of the kingdom of God. . . . We set the tone in our homes.

—*Petrea Kelly*

I'm having trouble managing the mansion. What I need is a wife.

—*Ella T. Grasso*

*B*ecause so many of us were young when our grandchildren were born, we've been a real part of their lives. We are even more experienced than their parents in communicating across the years. We got a lot of practice raising their parents and lowering our voices.

—*Lois Wyse*

*E*ducation concerning child abuse is essential to helping curb the problem. The church can play an important role by offering support and eventual healing for victims, as well as perpetrators. And equally important, while we're helping someone else, we can also help prevent it in our own families.

—*Ilene Dibble*

*W*e find some qualities in each other that we did not fully enjoy in our first marriages, and miss some we did enjoy. Yet we feel that everything we learn from each other will enable us eventually to build a union with the spouses to whom we are sealed that will be stronger than if Richard and I each had carried on alone in mortality. We know that our spouses are also learning and growing as they serve the Lord in another estate.

—*Marilyn Whipple*

I look into the faces of little children in any land and it reaffirms my belief that they are Heavenly Father's best gift to us.

—*Dwan J. Young*

*I*t is my greatest pleasure to serve the Lord in compassionate service by serving delicious meals to those in need.

—*Phyllis O. Sandberg*

*T*o listen to my friends, all grandchildren are superachievers.

—*Evelyn Bennett*

*T*he Lord has always done better for me than I could have done for myself. I had twelve children altogether. No, not altogether, just one at a time.

—*Ruth May Fox*

*F*am'lies can be together forever
Through Heav'nly Father's plan.

—*Ruth Muir Gardner*

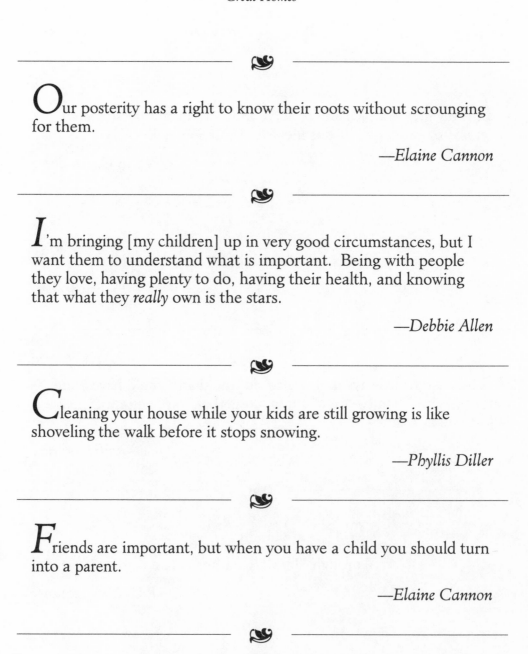

Our posterity has a right to know their roots without scrounging for them.

—*Elaine Cannon*

I'm bringing [my children] up in very good circumstances, but I want them to understand what is important. Being with people they love, having plenty to do, having their health, and knowing that what they *really* own is the stars.

—*Debbie Allen*

Cleaning your house while your kids are still growing is like shoveling the walk before it stops snowing.

—*Phyllis Diller*

Friends are important, but when you have a child you should turn into a parent.

—*Elaine Cannon*

*I*f a man is fortunate he will, before he dies, gather up as much as he can of his civilized heritage and transmit it to his children. And to his final breath he will be grateful for this inexhaustible legacy, knowing that it is our nourishing mother and our lasting life.

—*Ariel Durant*

*O*nce you've loved a child, you love all children. You give away your love to one, and find that by giving you have made yourself an inexhaustible treasury.

—*Margaret Lee Runbeck*

*T*he interviewer said, "Miss Lillian, what do you feel about your son, the President, telling small fibs—and just what is your definition of a small lie?"

"Well, do you remember when you first came in and I told you how nice you looked . . . ?"

—*Jimmy Carter's mother*

*G*od sends children to enlarge our hearts, and to make us unselfish and full of kindly sympathies and affections.

—*Mary Howitt*

*S*he could hear them living all through the house.

—*Great-grandma Spaulding*

*T*o my child:
You are the trip I did not take;
You are the pearls I did not buy;
You are my blue Italian lake;
You are my piece of foreign sky.

—*Anne Campbell*

*M*ost children never get over "blaming" parents, not even when they have children of their own. Gratitude comes after the grave. Why?

—*Madge Hennessy*

*F*or all the mistakes parents make—and their children will find them—my parents gave me an optimistic look at life: a lot of laughter.

—*Lucie Arnaz*

*I*f in marriage either part claims the right to stand supreme, to woman, the mother of the race, belongs the scepter, the crown. Her life is one long sacrifice for man.

—*Elizabeth Cody Stanton*

*D*ear Unforgettable Mother, We are doing fine, we have enough to eat. . . . It is hard for us because we have no family close by to go to.

—Elise Anderson, new immigrant

*W*hy do we encourage youngsters to become president when what we need are more garbage collectors?

—Julie Auchstetter

*E*ighty-nine percent of children in this country are in the public schools. They are supposed to be there many hours every week and 12 years of their lives. Those are formative years. What values are they learning? I believe they are learning values every hour of the day; there is no way to avoid that.

If they learn that you get ahead by doing your work neatly and accurately and on time, then those are the values they learn. If they learn that you are not punished if you steal other kids' lunch money, or you vandalize the lockers, or you sass the teachers, then they will learn those values. It's not a matter of having some "character education" course; it's a matter of what children absorb from all around them during their years at school.

—Phyllis Schiafly

*T*ake the pain out of change: when you move, it's a woman's job to put in place a few of your favorite things, and your new place will begin to feel like home.

—*Sue Christensen*

I see children as kites. You spend a lifetime trying to get them off the ground. You run with them until you're breathless. They crash, they hit the rooftop. You patch and comfort, adjust, and they'll fly. Finally, they are airborne. They need more string and you keep letting it out. But with each twist of the ball of twine there is a sadness that goes with joy. The kite becomes more distant, and you know it won't be long before that beautiful creature will snap the lifeline that binds you together, and will soar as it's meant to soar, free and alone. Only then will you know you have done your job.

—*Anonymous*

*T*he return to the uniquely sacred time in the Utah Mormon experience happens often enough to a large enough number of Latter-day Saints to guarantee that today's Saints live out their lives in a corporate community that still stands squarely and securely in the presence of the past.

—*Jan Shipps*

*T*o be a good cook you have to have a love of the good, a love of hard work, and a love of creating. Some people like to paint pictures, or do gardening, or build a boat in the basement. Other people get a tremendous pleasure out of the kitchen, because cooking is just as creative and imaginative an activity as drawing or wood carving, or music. And cooking draws upon your every talent—science, mathematics, energy, history, experience—and the more experience you have the less likely are your experiments to end in drivel and disaster. The more you know, the more you can create. There's no end to imagination in the kitchen.

—*Julia Child*

I live in gratitude to my parents for initiating me—and as early as I begged for it, without keeping me waiting—into knowledge of the word, into reading and spelling, by way of the alphabet. They taught it to me at home in time for me to begin to read before starting school.

My love for the alphabet, which endures, grew out of reciting it but, before that, out of seeing the letters on the page. In my own story books, before I could read them for myself I fell in love with various winding, enchanted-looking initials drawn by Walter Crane at the head of fairy tales. In "Once upon a time," an "o" had a rabbit running it as a treadmill, his feet upon flowers. When the day came years later for me to see the Book of Kells, all the wizardry of letter, initial, and word swept over me a thousand times, and the illumination, the gold, seemed a part of the world's beauty and holiness that had been there from the start.

—*Eudora Welty*

*M*other used to tell us, "I don't care if Heber J. Grant himself started smoking cigars—you won't!" So much for free agency, but it worked.

—*Nadine Cook*

*T*hey told me to talk about what it's like to have the priesthood in our house. But I don't really know. He's never home.

—*Holly Metcalf*

*T*hen Anna was born, so I had four babies to care for. But we got along very nice till the children got the scarlet fever. That was a hard year, but it passed on like all the rest.

—*Grandma Moses*

*T*he best conversations happen around our kitchen table. Many times we have laughed, cried, shared feelings, hopes and dreams; sorted out differences; solved the problems of the world; recognized our strengths and weaknesses into the wee hours of the morning.

—*Ruth B. Wright*

I understand more and more how true Daddy's words were when he said: All children must look after their own upbringing. Parents can only give good advice or put them on the right paths, but the final forming of a person's character lies in their own hands.

—*Anne Frank*

*S*aturday is a special day.
It's the day we get ready for Sunday:
We clean the house, and we shop at the store,
So we won't have to work until Monday.

—*Rita S. Robinson*

*T*he question is not, he notes, whether you can go home again, but whether you can ever leave. . . . Heritage follows relentlessly.

—*Claudia Bushman*

*L*et no crude act or word efface this sacred edifice of prayer.

—*Mabel Jones Gabbott*

*M*y mother . . . instilled within me the love for cooking. She has always been an inspiration to me, and when I am cooking I feel her closeness beside me, guiding and directing as I create.

—*Cecelia Ludwig*

*P*umpkins are fun to decorate, fun to cook, and fun to eat—and even vegetable-snubbing children agree. Even adults who eat plenty of vegetables should consider eating more pumpkin, for it couldn't be more nutritious, and it might even help curb your appetite.

—*Judith Ben Hurley*

A women who doesn't like kitchen duty isn't a female failure; she is a woman who doesn't like kitchen duty.

—*Elaine Cannon*

*M*y mother cooked for European royalty, and it has always been my intense desire to make all who sit at my table feel like royalty.

—*Cecelia Ludwig*

*C*ecelia Ludwig has revived within me the German heritage I have and has given me the desire to take time to learn and develop *that* cooking tradition—a delicious link of history that should never be forgotten.

—*Carrie B. Henderson*

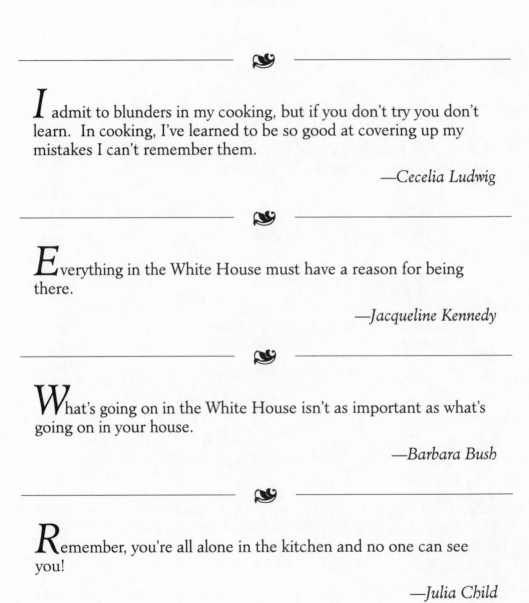

I admit to blunders in my cooking, but if you don't try you don't learn. In cooking, I've learned to be so good at covering up my mistakes I can't remember them.

—*Cecelia Ludwig*

*E*verything in the White House must have a reason for being there.

—*Jacqueline Kennedy*

*W*hat's going on in the White House isn't as important as what's going on in your house.

—*Barbara Bush*

*R*emember, you're all alone in the kitchen and no one can see you!

—*Julia Child*

*T*here was a time in my life when food was precious because it was scarce, so I learned to use everything—even celery leaves . . . and I learned to please the eye as well as the stomach in serving food. The plainest meal can be served attractively.

—*Cecelia Ludwig*

*W*hen your loved ones are in trouble, you fight for them. To me that is *not* heroic.

—*Lorraine Longbeck*

*W*e should write only letters of love, strength, and confidence in God to our missionaries.

—*Joanne Doxey*

*H*ow deep were the complexities of the everyday, of the family, what caves were in the mountains, what blocked chambers and what crystal rivers that had not yet seen the light.

—*Eudora Welty*

*T*raumas of childhood often mark the beginning of stamina for certain suffering in maturity.

—*Elaine Cannon*

*G*od must love housewives as he does the poor. He makes so many of us.

—*Phyllis McGinley*

*A*nd thank God for home-sweet things, a green
    and friendly hill,
And red geraniums aflame upon my window sill.

—*Martha Haskell Clark*

A woman's role is grand in the home: Whatever she teaches or does is going to be reflected in her children.

—*Maria Eugenia Aranda*

*T*he most important thing that happens when you tell a child a story is the close interaction that occurs between the two of you.

—*Deane Gage*

*A*nyone can leave money to their children, grandchildren, etc. But we are the only ones who can leave them our memories, and they are truly worth more than money.

—*Ethel Jackson Price*

*P*arenthood] is a learn-on-the-job situation. It's not for the faint-of-heart.

—*Kathleen "Casey" Null*

I recall a conversation with our youngest daughter, who was then a college sophomore. She said that her life had no meaning, she hated school, and she wanted out. She'd gone to school only to comply with her parents' wishes, she said, but now it was time for her to start making her own decisions. She needed her independence and autonomy.

"Okay," I said cautiously, "what do you plan to do?"

"Come home."

—*Maggie Scarf*

*H*aving family responsibilities and concerns just has to make you a more understanding person.

—*Sandra Day O'Connor*

I haven't put my mind in cold storage just because I have children.

—*Lisa Ramsey Adams*

I'm wife; I've finished that,
That other state;
I'm Czar, I'm woman now:
It's safer so.

—*Emily Dickinson*

*F*amilies are God's way of blessing the world, of shaping a strong, stubborn man into a strong, sensitive father, and a beautiful, bossy woman into a beautiful, blessed mother.

—*Elaine Cannon*

*L*et us be reminded that one of the great purposes of honoring mothers each year is to strengthen the moral and spiritual foundation of the family and home.

—*Joanne McKenna*

*T*here was a day in that pre-existent state when your Heavenly Father and mother gave you permission to leave your home there for awhile and come to earth.

—*Florence B. Pinnock*

*C*leanliness is next to godliness. The Spirit of God will not dwell in an unclean place—and that goes for your room as well as your body.

—*Florence S. Jacobsen*

*W*hat's more fun than all outdoors? Why, a winter picnic . . . an armload of firewood, plus this and that for outdoor cookery . . . kabobs, hot dogs, marshmallows, apples.

—*Shirley Paxman*

Where we have concern for others, the preparation for an occasion of any nature is something special . . . expense is not the key. People are inestimably more important than things.

—*Ruth H. Funk*

We were amused when our two-and-a-half-year-old daughter named her new doll Jennyology.

—*Susan Matsumura*

Compromising in marriage is not a call to sacrifice what is truly important to you. . . . Effective compromise is reached when both partners weigh their priorities and re-examine their solutions.

—*Kathy England*

*M*y own mother recorded some of her frustrations, and I am grateful for the written record of her "comings and goings". . . . She died when I was only six years old.

—*Wanda West Badger*

*E*ternal marriage is a daily decision, a daily act of love.

—*Kathy England*

*I*t takes a heap o' livin' in a house t' make it home"—and that's the truth.

—*Flora Amussen Benson*

*G*ive me a child until the age of six and I will make of him or her anything I will.

—*Dr. Dorothy Nyswander*

*T*o his Excellency Governor Carlin:

Sir: . . . We always have been, still are, and are determined always to be a law-abiding people. . . .

And now I appeal to your Excellency, as I would unto a father, who is not only able but willing to shield me and mine from every unjust prosecution. I appeal to your sympathies, and beg you to spare me and my helpless children. I beg you to spare my innocent children the heart-rending sorrow of again seeing their father unjustly dragged to prision, or to death. I appeal to your affections as a son, and beg you to spare our aged mother—the only surviving parent, we have left—the unsupportable affliction of seeing her son, whom she knows to be innocent of the crimes laid to his charge, thrown again into the hands of his enemies, who have so long sought for his life; in whose life and prosperity she only looks for the few remaining comforts she can enjoy. I entreat of your Excellency to spare us these afflictions and many sufferings which cannot be uttered, and secure to yourself the pleasure of doing good, and vastly increasing human happiness—secure to yourself the benediction of the aged, and the gratitude of the young, and the blessing and the veneration of the rising generation.

Respectfully, your most obedient,

—Emma Smith

*M*om's kind and clever
But a curious blend
Of an anxious mother
And a teen's best friend.

—*Kay Cammer*

I fell to thinking how all this blessedness of the attic came through me being curst. For if I hadna had a hare-lip to frighten me away into my own lonesome soul, this would never have come to me . . . for I should never have known the glory that came from the other side of silence.

Even while I was thinking this, out of nowhere suddenly came that lovely thing, and nestled in my heart, like a seed from the core of love.

—*Mary Webb*

*P*arents [are] accountable for their children's conduct . . . . Give them books and work to keep them from idleness . . . . Be full of love, goodness, and kindness. . . . Never do in secret, what [you] would not do in the presence of millions.

—*Lucy Mack Smith*

Growing

Neither here nor hereafter are we suddenly going to emerge with qualities of character and a level of living for which we have not prepared ourselves.

—Elaine Cannon

One of [my mother's] repeated admonitions, along with "Wipe your feet" and "Eat your asparagus," was "Don't go to bed until you've learned something new."

—Marilyn Arnold

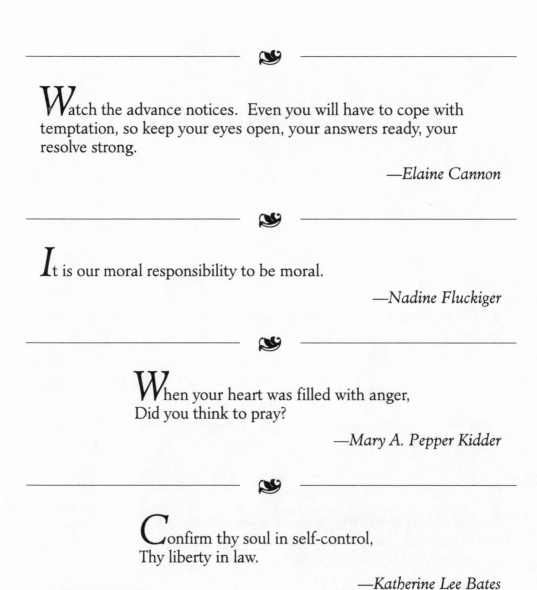

*W*atch the advance notices. Even you will have to cope with temptation, so keep your eyes open, your answers ready, your resolve strong.

—*Elaine Cannon*

*I*t is our moral responsibility to be moral.

—*Nadine Fluckiger*

*W*hen your heart was filled with anger,
Did you think to pray?

—*Mary A. Pepper Kidder*

*C*onfirm thy soul in self-control,
Thy liberty in law.

—*Katherine Lee Bates*

*F*irm as the mountains around us,
Stalwart and brave we stand
On the rock our fathers planted
For us in this goodly land.

—*Ruth May Fox*

*I*f you are going to write about your days, you had better be doing something to write about.

—*Caroline Eyring Miner*

*U*nhappiness is bad for the health.

—*Anna Greenwood*

*T*hose who dwell, as scientists or laymen, among beauties and mysteries of the earth are never alone or weary of life. Those who contemplate the beauty of the earth find reserves of strength that will endure as long as life lasts. There is something infinitely healing in the repeated refrains of nature—the assurance that dawn comes after night and spring after winter.

—*Rachel Carson*

*Y*a gotta wanna win! . . . Stop waiting for someone to make your day. Make your own day.

—*Suzanne L. Hansen*

*W*ith this move, we'll start another tomorrow.

—*Irene Buchner*

*S*ince skills obsolesce and facts wear out, the best gift in today's world is a love of the act of learning. There is a knack to learning. You are never too young to acquire it. Enjoy it and it becomes a habit. Then you are constantly becoming ready for work that does not yet exist. Life always opens out . . . in a pathway of eternal progression.

—Mabel S. Noall

*T*here's a belief that teenagers are victims of their hormones. Some people seem to think that the hormones coursing through your bloodstream are responsible for everything you say or do. . . . It would be convenient to blame everything . . . disconcerting or unpredictable . . . on hormones. Don't—you ultimately make a conscious decision about what you will and will not do.

—Debra Kent

*T*he best answers are the ones you discover within yourself.

—Margaret Smoot

*A*dversity proves whom God can trust. Adversity gives us experience. Adversity brings us closer to the Lord.

—*Elaine Cannon*

*F*ace your danger in time. Face your danger with courage and faith, and with the will to survive. Every crucial experience can be a setback, or a new start.

—*Mary Roberts Rinehart*

*T*he development and the testing of our faith and patience require time. If prayers for the relief of our burdens were answered too quickly, there would be no time for the long-suffering, the soul stretching, or the healing balm of the repentance to take place.

—*Mary Flint Foulger*

*S*oliloquy is an important part of my growing. . . . By taking time daily to think through my plans, desires, hopes, frustrations, needs, and anguish I find that I can sort out the flowers from the weeds for that day.

—Elaine Reiser Alder

*O*ne learns to accept the fact that no permanent return is possible to an old form of relationship; and, more deeply still, that there is no holding of a relationship to a single form. This is not a tragedy but part of the ever-recurrent miracle of life and growth.

—Anne Morrow Lindbergh

*I*n all occupations that were previously closed to women, the blatant barriers have been removed *before* the environment has substantially changed. The behaviors and attitudes always lag behind.

—Sharyn Lenhart

*I*t is easy to do again what you shouldn't have done before.

—*Una Dastrup*

I who am blind can give one hint to those who see: Use your eyes as if tomorrow you would be stricken blind. And the same method can be applied to the other senses. Hear the music of voices, the song of a bird, the mighty strains of an orchestra, as if you would be stricken deaf tomorrow. Touch each object as if tomorrow your tactile sense would fail. Smell the perfume of flowers, taste with relish each morsel, as if tomorrow you could never smell and taste again. Make the most of every sense; glory in the beauty which the world in all the facets of pleasure reveals to you through the several means of contact which Nature provides. But of all the senses, I am sure that sight is the most delightful.

—*Helen Keller*

*I*f you have made a mistake and don't correct it, you are making another mistake.

—*Elaine Cannon*

*W*ould you be interesting? Read. Would you know the best thoughts of the greatest people? Read. Would you know the greatest events in the countries of the world? Read. Would you know the earth and its peoples? Read. Would you know the gospel of Jesus Christ? Read. And with all your reading follow the advice of the wise Abbe Diment who said that we mustn't be content with reading good books; life is too short; we must read only the best.

—Marba C. Josephson

*Y*ou can't grow up until you forgive.

—Jane Fonda

*C*onsider education not as the painful accumulation of facts and dates and reigns, nor merely the necessary preparation of the individual to earn his keep in the world, but as the transmission of our mental, moral, technical, and aesthetic heritage as fully as possible to as many as possible, for the enlargement of man's understanding, control, embellishment, and enjoyment of life.

—Ariel Durant

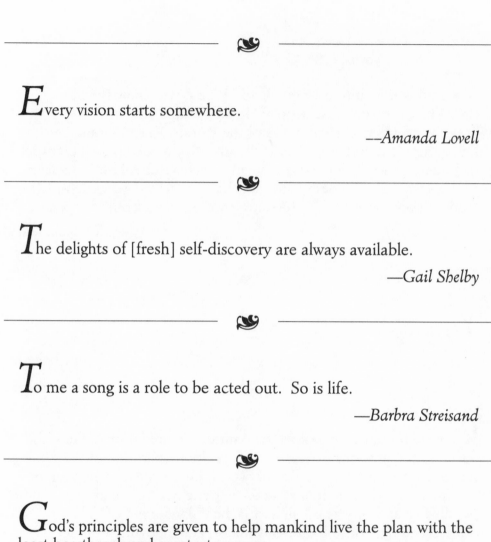

*E*very vision starts somewhere.

—*Amanda Lovell*

*T*he delights of [fresh] self-discovery are always available.

—*Gail Shelby*

*T*o me a song is a role to be acted out. So is life.

—*Barbra Streisand*

*G*od's principles are given to help mankind live the plan with the least heartbreak and greatest success.

—*Elaine Cannon*

Not knowing how to feed the spirit, we try to muffle its demands in distraction. . . . What matters is that one be for a time inwardly attentive.

—*Anne Morrow Lindbergh*

Those who take rides on rainbows and hear music from dusty violins know that life is a many-splendoured thing.

—*Flavia*

While we may not truly be masters of our own destiny, considering the forces of evil, accident, and illness which may alter the course we chart for ourselves—we are masters of the attitudes which shape our destiny. If our behavior is dictated by fear, we are handing outside forces responsibility for our destiny.

—*Marilyn Drumright*

*L*et there be many windows to your soul,
That all the glory of the universe
May beautify it. . . .
And all the forces of the firmament
Shall fortify your strength.

—*Ella Wheeler Wilcox*

*I*mportant: When we can begin to take our failures non-seriously, it means we are ceasing to be afraid of them. It is of immense importance to learn to laugh at ourselves.

—*Katherine Mansfield*

*C*ourage is the price that life extracts for granting peace. The soul that knows it not, knows no release from little things.

—*Amelia Earhart*

I live a full and busy life. Only sometimes I feel a haunting sadness. At dusk, when day is fading away and the level of my physical energies is at a low ebb, I may find myself depressed and nostalgic. But the next morning I invariably wake up with renewed optimism and welcome the day as another opportunity given me by God for enlightenment and experience.

—*Nien Cheng*

*O*ne ship drives east and another drives west
With the selfsame winds that blow.
    'Tis the set of the sails
    And not the gales
Which tells us the way to go.

Like the winds of the sea are the ways of fate,
    As we voyage along through life:
    'Tis the set of a soul
    That decides its goal,
And not the calm or the strife.

—*Ella Wheeler Wilcox*

*T*o acquire is not enough. One must also know how to conserve and skillfully manage if all is to go well.

—*Cecelia Ludwig*

*O*ne of our greatest needs is to recognize the good from the past that should be preserved and protected and to see the good from the present that should be embraced and encouraged.

—*Barbara B. Smith*

*A*lmost half of all Americans today are descendants of Ellis Island immigrants. Ellis processed 5,000 people a day in the early 1900's. The reasons people came to America were varied, but they all shared hope for a better life—and their dreams fueled America's greatness.

—*Linda Rosenberg*

*A*n 1876 school girl received a note pinned on her work: "Before 1530,
t h e r e w a s n o p u n c t u a t i o n i n w r i t i n g andsowhatdoyouthinkitlookedlikeyouarerightitlookedlikethis. Kindly correct."

—*Retrenchment Association leader*

*N*o one else is so well prepared to amuse and entertain the young as the young themselves when they are directed by proper authority.

—*Susa Young Gates*

I learned organization as the mother of a four-year-old and newborn twins. I never got over it. I still read things, and I write down little bits of information, for later use.

—*Mary Ellen Jordon Haight*

*W*hen winter comes you can see which trees stay green. In life, bitter days prove the soul's steadfastness.

—*Paula Westcott*

*T*he beauty of work depends upon the way we meet it; whether we arm ourselves each morning to attack it as an enemy that must be vanquished before night comes—or whether we open our eyes with the sunrise to welcome it as an approaching friend who will make us feel at evening the day was well worth its fatigue.

—*Lucy Larcom*

*T*he best cosmetic in the world is an active mind that is always finding something new.

—*Mary Meek Atkeson*

Women people are depressed, they can't always tell right from wrong.

—*Ethel Adelman*

Women aren't encouraged to go into science because it is perceived as cold and masculine. Women are heavily represented in biology because it has to do with "life" and is considered to be warmer. But I find physics to be very beautiful.

—*Nai-chang Yeh*

Oh, stop whining!

—*Paula Witteman*

*T*here is always a value in striving, always compensation for effort. When these efforts have an aim to relieve and bless, the result is a gain in priceless experience and a growth in spiritual power.

—*Louise Y. Robison*

*F*or I am my mother's daughter, and the dreams of Africa still beat in my heart. They will not let me rest while there is a single Negro boy or girl without a chance to prove his worth.

—*Mary McLeod Bethune*

*N*o matter what your heartache is, don't let your heart shut down.

—*Marilyn Van Derbur*

*S*ome people get so broadminded all their brains fall out.

—*Minnie Egan Anderson*

*E*ach trial in life can be the catalyst to our celestial potential.

—*Geri Walton*

I have searched the scriptures under topics such as despair and bitterness. I found in Hebrews 12:15 that roots of bitterness can trouble and defile us if we don't watch carefully.

—*Joan Leavitt*

*T*rials and adversity are difficult for all of us. . . . Attitude is everything. Support from others will likely be forthcoming if we *decide* to be pleasant.

—*Patrice Harris*

I did not realize until recently that commandments are not tethers to bind us down but are guidelines to true happiness.

—*Sandie Blair*

*L*ife begins tomorrow. . . . Put much ahead of you; then you need not covet what you have left behind.

—*Ardis Whitman*

I see you . . . caught up in the excitement of doing good deeds and making wise choices . . . learning, growing, and feeling at home with the beauties of the world . . . reaching out and gathering those who may be weaker.

—*Ardeth G. Kapp*

*E*xert thy will and use for self-control
God gave thee jurisdiction of thy soul.
All thine immortal powers bring into play;
Think, act, strive, reason, and look up and pray.

—*Ella Wheeler Wilcox*

*B*e possessed of good judgment . . . the faculty of placing everything in its proper place . . . discernment, reason, moderation, consistency, wisdom.

—*Katie C. Jensen*

*O*h, to learn that sore seasons are sent to teach obedience, and that the best obedience stems not from "I must!" but from "I believe—consequently I trust."

—*Denise Tucker*

*L*et me not through human hesitation forfeit my right to Heavenly Inspiration.

—*Gail Christensen*

*A*s long as we are willing, God will make us able.

—*Connie Nelson*

*P*eople aren't perfect—not even prophets.

—*Camilla Eyring Kimball*

*S*uccess, happiness, and even salvation may be a simple matter of being prepared and in the right place at the right time.

—*Emily H. Bennett*

*H*is lofty soul comprehended the grandeur of his mission on earth, and with divine fortitude he fulfilled the destiny which God had ordained for him before the world was. . . . So must we.

—*Velma Johnson*

*M*ountains and mind are conquerable within books.

—*Donna Toland Smart*

*D*o you think your candle is getting dim? Remember, you are stronger than I thought!

—*Blanche Miles*

*L*et's have traveling libraries. . . . Many wards have libraries, but the books, being once read, are left idle. By boxing them and sending them out to other wards, they can become useful again.

—*Ruth May Fox*

Giving

Compassionate service? Bea not only believed in it, she lived it. It was while I slept under heavy medication that Bea came to our property and picked the ripe peaches. The next day she returned with nearly sixty quarts of fruit fit, to my marveling eyes, for the state fair exhibit. Only another woman knows the work behind that kind of project. Our family ate bottled peaches with a special kind of reverence all that winter.

—*Elaine Cannon*

What sets our choir apart is that we have a special message of hope and love to give to a needy world.

—*Rita Jensen*

*T*he world is moved along, not only by the mighty shoves of its heroes, but also by the aggregate of the tiny pushes of each honest worker.

—*Helen Keller*

*W*hat do we live for if not to make life less difficult for each other.

—*Mary Ann Evans*

*I*n the nineteenth century, most people thought of educating blacks only to read the Bible. And *nobody* thought of educating Indians.

—*Minnie Cassatt Hickman*

*G*ive to the world the best you have and the best will come back to you.

—*Mary de Vere*

Go and toil in any vineyard,
 Do not fear to do or dare;
If you want a field of labor,
 You can find it anywhere.

—*Ellen M. H. Gates*

There are two kinds of people on earth today,
Just two kinds of people, no more, I say. . . .

. . . the two kinds of people on earth I mean
Are the people who lift and the people who lean.

—*Ella Wheeler Wilcox*

Give man the breastplate courage plies,
But give to woman fortitude.

—*Eliza R. Snow*

*Y*esterday, when we went out for a walk, an older man came over to meet me. "A comrade," my mother whispered, taking my hand and placing it in his. These people have lived their whole lives caring about the world. Little by little the dogma has dropped away, and now only the sense of human possibility remains. It makes them tender, in spite of their militancy.

—Kim Cheriun

*H*aving compassion on those who are hurting for whatever reason and then translating the response of the heart into the needed act is truly ministering as God would have us do.

—Joy F. Evans

*L*ove has nothing to do with what you are expecting to get—only with what you are expecting to give—which is everything. . . . You give because you love and you cannot help giving. If you are very lucky, you may be loved back. That is delicious but it does not necessarily happen.

—Katharine Hepburn

*T*here may have been someone who could have done more to help me along, though I doubt it; what I needed was cheering, and always before they had let me plod onward without it. You helped refashion the dream of my heart, and made me turn eagerly to it.

—*Grace Strickes Dawson*

*I*t seems to me I discovered what "I love you" really means. It means I put you and your interests and your comfort ahead of my own interest and my own comfort because I love you.

—*Katharine Hepburn*

*D*uring the Gulf War eleven Iraqis surrendered to a reporter, who directed them to a prisoner of war camp.
   "You see the most wonderful kindnesses under pressure. It's a picture for any journalist."

—*Elizabeth O. Colton*

*I*t is better to light a candle than to curse the darkness.

—*Eleanor Roosevelt*

*L*et's have compassion without the casserole.

—*Evelyn Bennett*

*Y*ou can drag the children to church but you can't make them listen—unless you are prepared.

—*LaVern Parmalee*

*I*t is suicidal for our wealthy nation to allow children to grow up in poverty. High child poverty rates make it difficult to solve social problems such as substance abuse, crime, teenage pregnancy, and poor academic performance. The problems . . . ultimately can affect older Americans directly.

—*Marian Wright Edelman*

A church is for the purpose of changing and strengthening lives, but it can change people's lives for good only if it teaches truth. Christ's church changed lives because its truths changed attitudes.

—*Nadine Cook*

I haven't married—yet—but I am productive and happy as long as I keep an eternal perspective.

—*Phyllis Roundy*

*G*ive me good health and I'll take care of the rest. . . . It takes a lot of guts to sing all of this difficult music.

—*Marilyn Horne*

*L*ove is something like the clouds that were in the sky before the sun came out. You cannot touch the clouds, you know; but you feel the rain and know how glad the flowers and the thirsty earth are to have it after a hot day. You cannot touch love either; but you feel the sweetness that it pours into everything.

—*Annie Sullivan*

I long to accomplish a great and noble task, but it is my chief duty to accomplish small tasks as if they were great and noble.

—*Helen Keller*

*T*he spirit within you remains a free thing filled with boundless dreams to share.

—*Flavia*

*B*ecause of severe scarring from burns I suffered as a child I became overweight. From my pain came my quest to be a healer and builder of people, especially the outcasts, the unaccepted.

—*Lorraine Mauderscheid*

*I*f I had known what trouble you were bearing;
What griefs were in the silence of your face;
I would have been more gentle, and more caring,
And tried to give you gladness for a space.

—*Mary Carolyn Davies*

*T*his I learned from the shadow of a tree,
That to and fro did sway against a wall:
Our shadow selves, our influence, may fall
Where ourselves can never be.

—*Anna G. Hamilton*

*T*he sweet influence of the Relief Society work, has been to hundreds of our sisters a consolation in passing through trying ordeals.

—*Emmeline B. Wells*

*H*ow proud we are to perform this service for our suffering and glorious cause. Our hearts and prayers go with the gifts which we have laid upon the altar of our country.

—*Clarissa S. Williams*

*H*ow can we help our [young people] live by the standards of the Church? . . . Help them differentiate between vulgar and merely awkward dancing.

—*Lucy Grant Cannon*

*S*hame on you if your house is dusted, and a neighbor needs help.

—Katie Jensen

*T*he Lord knows what our situations are and he will support us and give us grace and strength for the day if we continue to put our trust in him and devote ourselves unreservedly to his service.

—Mary Fielding Smith

*B*eyond ourselves, beyond our family circles, we have responsibility . . . to feed his lambs and give them an understanding of their real worth and eternal potential.

—Dwan J. Young

*I*t is very gratifying to see dedicated women helping their sisters wherever they may be.

—*Ann S. Reese*

*A*nd what if God was as we are—too busy with burdens of his own to lend a helping hand? Oh, what if . . . ?

—*Elaine Cannon*

*W*hat can I give Him
Poor as I am?
If I were a shepherd,
I would give Him a lamb,
If I were a Wise Man,
I would do my part,—
But what I can I give Him,
Give my heart.

—*Christina G. Rossetti*

*W*e have to give children opportunities to make decisions, to give love and service until they know how to do it on their own.

—*Dwan J. Young*

Geniality

*B*eing loved is flattering. An exchange—where love is received, and also returned—is God's gift.

—*Elaine Cannon*

*A*s long as there are negotiations there is hope for good relations.

—*Norma B. Smith*

*H*appiness and peace are found when we are in harmony with ourselves, with God, and with our fellowmen.

—*Barbara W. Winder*

Who am I to judge another
When I walk imperfectly?

—Susan Evans McCloud

Love cannot be forced, love cannot be coaxed and teased. It comes out of Heaven, unasked and unsought.

—Pearl S. Buck

Of courtesy, it is much less
Than courage of heart or holiness,
Yet in my walks it seems to me
That the Grace of God is in courtesy.

—Hilaire Belloc

*U*nless you can die when the dream is past—
Oh never call it love!

—*Dinah Maria Mulock Craik*

*T*he more one loves, the stronger becomes the capacity for loving, and it is the hands that are always busy with helpfulness that always find yet more to do.

—*Maud Ballington Booth*

*S*hould you happen to notice that another person is extremely tall or overweight, eats too much or declines convivial drinks, ought to be married or ought not to be pregnant—see if you can refrain from bringing these astonishing observations to that person's attention.

—*Judith Martin*

God has been very gracious to me, for I never dwell upon anything wrong which a person has done, so as to remember it afterwards. If I do remember it, I always see some other virtue in that person.

—*St. Theresa of Avila*

To be alive in such an age! . . .
When men speak strong for brotherhood,
For peace and universal good,
When miracles are everywhere,
And every inch of common air
Throbs a tremendous prophecy
Of greater marvels yet to be.
     O thrilling age,
     O willing age!

—*Angela Morgan*

*A*ll modern life makes for social responsibility. . . . We have learned that our own interests can be secure only in the security of our neighbor's.

—*Margaret E. Sangster*

*L*earn what love means. Be kind to one another and to everyone around. Kindness is the music of the world.

—*Louise Lake*

*T*he reason for my starting a diary is that I have no real friend.

—*Anne Frank*

*O*h, the comfort—the inexpressible comfort of feeling safe with a person.

—*Dinah Maria Mulock Craik*

*S*ome people succumb to the taunt [of the crowd] because they are not converted enough to their own beliefs of right to give them the power they need.

—*Caroline Eyring Miner*

I'm struggling to enjoy the blessings of the gospel once again. The transition would be easier if I felt support from friends, family, and members. While not all less-active members will desire what I do, it's hard for anyone to keep rejecting sincere, unconditional love. So reach out to a less-active member who may or may not know he or she is saying, "Touch my heart."

—*Name withheld upon request*

*N*obody sees a flower—really—it is so small we haven't time— and to see takes time like to have a friend takes time.

—*Georgia O'Keefe*

*I*f I had known in the morning
    How wearily all the day
The words unkind would trouble my mind
    That I said when you went away,
I had been more careful, darling,
    Nor given you needless pain;
But we vex our own with look and tone
    We may never take back again.

              —*Margaret E. Sangster*

I am my own.
And howsoever near my friend may draw
Unto my soul, there is a legend hung
Above a certain straight and narrow way
Says "Dear my friend, ye may not enter here!"

              —*Barbara Young*

*T*he hands of those I meet are dumbly eloquent to me. The touch of some hands is an impertinence. I have met people so empty of joy that when I clasped their frosty fingertips, it seemed as if I were shaking hands with a northeast storm. Others there are whose hands have sunbeams in them, so that their grasp warms my heart.

—*Helen Keller*

*B*ehind the red facade of war and politics, misfortune and poverty, adultery and divorce, murder and suicide, were millions of orderly homes, devoted marriages, men and women kindly and affectionate, troubled and happy with children. Even in recorded history we find so many instances of goodness, even of nobility, that we can forgive, though not forget, the sins.

—*Ariel Durant*

*T*he main dangers in this life are the people who want to change everything . . . or nothing.

—*Lady Astor*

*T*he most beautiful discovery true friends make is that they can grow separately without growing apart.

—*Elisabeth Foley*

*T*here is an enormous difference between love and like. Usually we use the word "love" when we really mean like. I think very few people ever mean love, I think that like is a much easier relationship. It is based on sense.

—*Katharine Hepburn*

*H*ow much quicker we are to find fault and speak of what annoys us than of that which is pleasant and cheerful. How much plainer people's faults show than their virtues.

—*Mary Jane Mount Tanner*

*T*he emotional or physical abuse of one human being by another is absolutely unacceptable. The offender who breaks the laws of God and the laws of the land by inflicting abuse on any level should be dealt with just as others are who break covenants and commit grievous sexual sins.

—*Elaine Cannon*

*N*othing is menial where there is love.

—*Pearl S. Buck*

I'm with [the artist] who created the famous poster of the sixties, "What if they gave a war and nobody came?" It still applies.

—*Grethe Peterson*

*N*ever put yourselves among a pleasure-loving group on Sunday.

—*Martha H. Tingey*

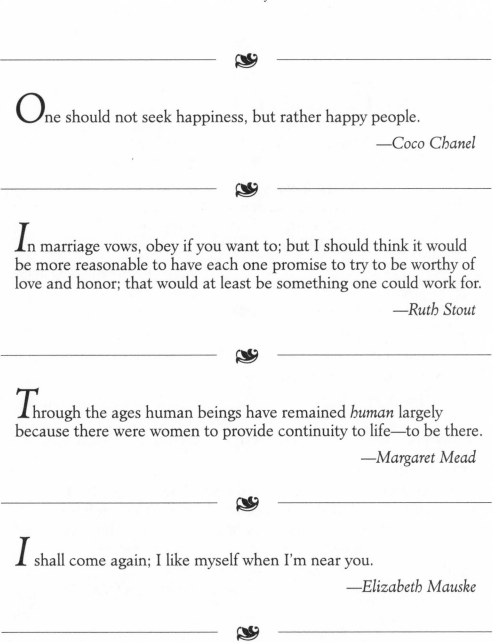

One should not seek happiness, but rather happy people.

—*Coco Chanel*

In marriage vows, obey if you want to; but I should think it would be more reasonable to have each one promise to try to be worthy of love and honor; that would at least be something one could work for.

—*Ruth Stout*

Through the ages human beings have remained *human* largely because there were women to provide continuity to life—to be there.

—*Margaret Mead*

I shall come again; I like myself when I'm near you.

—*Elizabeth Mauske*

*F*or friendship holds a secret cord,
    That with the fibres of my heart,
Entwines so deep, so close, 'tis hard
    For death's dissecting hand to part!

I feel the low responses roll,
    Like the far echo of the night,
And whisper, softly through my soul,
    "I would not be forgotten quite."

—*Eliza R. Snow*

*T*he greatest determiner of human happiness is whether or not we have someone to love and confide in.

—*Dr. Joyce Brothers*

*T*he next time the children started quarreling, I fought back an urge to get angry and started singing, "Jesus said love everyone; treat them kindly too. When your heart is filled with love, others will love you." Both children stopped quarreling and looked up in happy surprise. Mother was singing!

—*Margery D. Small*

*I*t isn't only important for each of us to be of service to others, but it is equally as important to be gracious receivers, to allow others the blessings that come from serving.

—*Janeen Hullinger*

*E*xcerpt from a letter to President Gordon B. Hinckley, read at general conference:
   "Please remind the brethren that the physical and verbal abuse of women is inexcusable, never acceptable, and a cowardly way of dealing with differences."

—*Name withheld*

*I*t appears that when the abuse is chronic, when the perpetrator [of abuse] is a family member, when secrecy is coerced, and when force or terror is used, children suffer greater emotional damage.

—*Carolyn Newberger, Ed. D.*

I think the only thing people are interested in is people. I think it's a star-struck nation.

—*Diana Vreeland*

*M*y life cannot implement in action the demands of all the people to whom my heart responds.

—*Anne Morrow Lindbergh*

*W*e don't need a bishop's assignment to be kind. We don't need to sign up to be thoughtful.

—*Chieko N. Okazaki*

I sheath my sword. In mercy go.
    Turn back from me your hopeless eyes,
    For in them all my anger dies:
I cannot face a beaten foe.

My cause was just, the fight was sweet.
    Go from me, O mine enemy,
    Before, in shame of victory,
You find me kneeling at your feet.

—Aline Kilmer

I gradually lost my hostility . . . and learned to respect the great number of people who came forward to help minorities find their place on the campus.

—Alberta Henry

*W*hat we think, how we act, what we say—our attitudes—determine [our] face value.

—LaRue Longden

Gentlemen

*M*en are marvelous—just ask them.

—*Elaine Cannon*

*H*ave thou nothing to do with that just man.

—*Pilate's wife*

*F*ew things are more pleasing to see than a grateful heart wrapped up in a young person. It's a pleasure to be with him; it's a joy to do things for him!

—*Winnifred C. Jardine*

———————— 🌿 ————————

I don't want to spend all of his money—just most of it!

—*Cheryle Cummings*

———————— 🌿 ————————

*L*ook at that fat carry-on bag of his. . . . He's like an American Express card—don't leave home without it.

—*Maxine Mertzel*

———————— 🌿 ————————

*A*bstinence makes your life grow stronger.

—*Elaine Cannon*

———————— 🌿 ————————

*P*roviding women with money could well be the only way many men know how to give. If they believe we would prefer to be bought off, how much less anxiety they must feel about giving affection.

—*Georgia Witkin, Ph.D.*

———————— 🌿 ————————

*E*very woman should have a husband like mine.

—*Geneva Brown*

*W*hen the princely weaver kisses Prudence Sarn upon the spot of her deformity [a hare-lip] it does not go away, she does not shed it suddenly. Rather, the blemish, loved and kissed at last, can make her whole and open up the gates of entry to the joys it threatened to deny.

—*Erika Duncan*

I've chosen my bit of Paradise. 'Tis on your breast, my dear acquaintance!"

—*Mary Webb*

Do I love you? Haven't I shared your bed, washed your shirts, made your meals for twenty-five years?

—*Golda, Tevye's wife*

In passing . . . I would like to say that the first time Adam had a chance he laid the blame on women.

—*Nancy Astor*

A talk-show host asked me why Fang and I were getting a divorce. I told him it was because of that book he brought to bed every night. He said a lot of people read in bed. I said reading was one thing, but the coloring jiggled the bed so much I couldn't sleep.

—*Phyllis Diller*

*I*f it was possible to hate one time more than another in camp, I hated Christmas. . . . The Japanese office sent word that we were to meet our husbands for half an hour, in the field outside the barracks. . . . We sat with our husbands quietly under the trees. They held their children lovingly to them, and yearned over them. But the children would not have much of that. They were outside the barbed wire today, in the field with the trees and the stream running wild, climbing trees and . . . running free. Fathers were secondary to freedom. . . . At the end of half an hour the parting came. As always, I felt that I had forgotten the most important thing. . . . I had talked of this and that and anxiety, when all that I should have said was, I love you.

—*Agnes Newton Keith*

*W*ait, Karl—before you leave—let me put my arms around you!

—*Virginia Solomon*

*I*n the ever-widening circles of single women and of women weary of juggling two jobs—at home and the workplace—polygamy begins to look better . . . not because the men are so great but the women are.

—*Johanna Jarvik*

*T*he day I turned away from my own dreams to support my husband in his unselfish service to others was a beginning in a long life of coming to grips with priorities, of balancing along the fine line between good choices and better ones.

—*Elaine Cannon*

*O*ne never realizes how different a husband and wife can be until they begin to pack for a trip.

—*Erma Bombeck*

*T*wo shall be born, the whole wide world apart, and speak in different tongues and have no thought each of the other's being and notice. . . . One day out of darkness they shall meet and read life's meaning in each other's eyes.

—Susan Marr Spalding

*W*e never spoke of ordinary things . . . my farm or his work.

—Isak Dinesen

*A*ri promised that, if I'm good, next year he'll give me the moon.

—Jacqueline Kennedy

*O*h, Jerry, let's not ask for the moon when we have the stars.

—Bette Davis (in Now, Voyager*)*

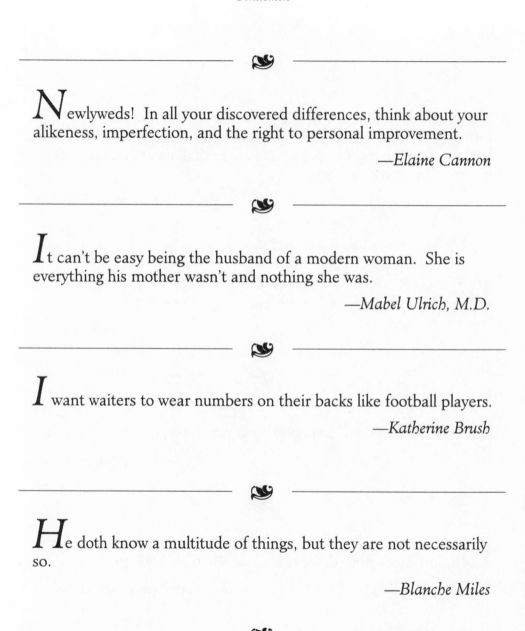

*N*ewlyweds! In all your discovered differences, think about your alikeness, imperfection, and the right to personal improvement.

—*Elaine Cannon*

*I*t can't be easy being the husband of a modern woman. She is everything his mother wasn't and nothing she was.

—*Mabel Ulrich, M.D.*

I want waiters to wear numbers on their backs like football players.

—*Katherine Brush*

*H*e doth know a multitude of things, but they are not necessarily so.

—*Blanche Miles*

*S*arah laughed within herself, saying, After I am waxed old shall I have pleasure, my lord being old also?

—*Sarah, Abraham's wife*

I have long felt that modesty in dress and behavior are virtues as attractive in men as in women, and I wish there would be a comeback in such refinement as there has been in opera.

—*Elaine Cannon*

I very sincerely wish you would control yourself so as to keep all your matters in order yourself without depending upon others, as that is the only way to be happy, to have all your business in your own hands.

—*Martha Washington*

*T*he web [of marriage] is fashioned of love. Yes, but many kinds of love: romantic love first, then slow-growing devotion, and playing through these, a constantly rippling relationship. It is made of loyalties and interdependencies and shared experiences. It is woven of memories of meetings and conflicts; of triumphs and disappointments. It is a web of communication, a common language, and the acceptance of lack of language, too.

—Anne Morrow Lindbergh

*H*elen always thought that when Harry left her, it would be in a pine box. Instead he departed in a late-model Porsche with a late-model product manager in his company.

—Lois Wyse

*H*e must be certain not only that he abandoned the sin but that he has changed the situations surrounding the sin. He should avoid the places and conditions and circumstances where the sin occurred, for these could most readily breed it again. He must abandon the people with whom the sin was committed. He may not hate the persons involved, but he must avoid them and everything associated with the sin. He must dispose of all letters, trinkets, and things which will remind him of the "old days" and the "old times." He must forget addresses, telephone numbers, people, places, situations from the sinful past and build a new life. He must eliminate anything which would stir the old memories . . . and I must forgive him.

—*Wife of a wayward husband*

*A*s for ambitions, mine are destined to be much more fully satisfied than ever yours will be, because, you see, I am so fully satisfied by what you do while you will never be. By the same rule how much greater is my delight in your triumphs than it could ever have been in any little success of my own.

—*Ellen Wilson*

Going to him? Happy letter! Tell him.
Tell him the page I didn't write;
Tell him I said the syntax
And left the verb and pronoun out.

—Emily Dickinson

We read in the evening and are silent for hours; at moments I glance at him or he at me with a pleasant smile ever with joy. I am very happy—winning him by my kindness and meekness.

—Anna Dostoevsky

I had many times said with much earnestness that if a husband ever came home to me drunken and abusive as some men . . . did to their wives, "I would kill him." And I full believed that I would do it. Though I knew that no murderer could enter the celestial kingdom.

—Martha Cragun Cox

*A*ll the time you were at war, son, I just got on my knees here by this bed and told the Lord about you, told Him how I felt about you and the kind of man you are and my dreams and aspirations for you. I asked Him to preserve you from evil, and to help you do your duty for your country courageously. Then I climbed into bed and left you in His hands and went to sleep.

—*Maude F. Hanks*

*S*ome people assume I'm against young romance. There's not a bit of truth in it. But hanky panky is out, and in 1962 when sexual freedom increased on campuses, I called a compulsory assembly and told our 1,450 Vassar girls to stay chaste or leave the campus.

—*Sarah Gibson Blanding*

*R*esolved, that realizing ourselves to be wives and daughters of apostles, prophets, and elders of Israel, and as such that high responsibilities rest upon us . . . we do mutually pledge ourselves that we will uphold and sustain each other in doing good.

—*Eliza R. Snow*

*I*t was truley gratifying to see the venerabl[e] Patriarch [Joseph Smith, Sr.] with his two aged Brothers in the upper stand and in the next, four of his Sons with president Rigdon in their midst, all I believe faithful servants of the living God. Joseph & Hirum I know best and love much. While I lookd at them all my heart was drawn out in earnest prayer and to our heavenly Father in their behalf and also for the Prophetice their aged Mother [Lucy Mack Smith] whose eyes are frequently baithed in tears when she looks at, or speaks of them.

—Mary Fielding Smith

*B*e not unequally yoked together. . . . Be warned that there are . . . wolves in sheep's clothing . . . going stealthily about seeking the innocent, unsuspecting victims, pursuing their prey with a fixed purpose to destroy.

—Susa Young Gates

I well recollect the sensations with which my mind was actuated when I learned the fact that my husband had been called and ordained to the Melchizedek Priesthood and would undoubtedly be required to travel and preach the gospel to the nations of the earth. I realized in some degree the immense responsibility of the office, and besought the Lord for grace and wisdom to be given him that he might be able to magnify his high and holy calling.

—*Caroline Barnes*

*M*y husband has been laid upon his bed for the space of two days and two nights; and some say that he is not dead, but others say that he is dead and that he stinketh, and that he ought to be placed in the sepulchre; but as for myself, to me he doth not stink.

—*King Lamoni's wife*

*V*isionary man . . . Behold thou hast led us forth from the land of our inheritance, . . . and we perish in the wilderness.

—*Sariah, Lehi's wife*

A good marriage—which means a continually improving marriage—is a spiritual experience, not a kind of glandular fever.

—*Virginia Baldwin*

A simple rule to [teach your sons] regarding sexual harassment: "If you can't say (or do) it to your mother, wife, or sister in public, don't say (or do) it to any other woman."

—*Mary Chandler*

*T*evye's wife considered washing his shirts and making his meals—even "sharing" his bed—to be love. It isn't—it is dutiful housekeeping.

—*Barbara Stoker*

*I*f it were left to the men to get the Primary talks memorized, shoes found, hair curled, dinner prepared—the family would never get to church. But my husband says it can't be helped—men have to shave every day.

—*Elaine Cannon*

*W*hen Harvard men say they have graduated from Radcliffe, then we've made it.

—*Jacqueline Kennedy*

*W*e women may talk too much for the comfort of men, but even then we don't tell half we know.

—*Elaine Cannon*

*M*en mature. Women grow obsolete.

—*LaRue Longden*

A woman needs another point of view—she should marry.

—*Bertha Reeder*

A clever woman can turn a man into a lamb in one moment and convince him he's king of beasts the next.

—*Mary Jane Johnson*

*N*ever forget the real difference between men and women. A man comes home from a trip and tosses his dirty laundry. A woman comes home from a trip and does it.

—*Elaine Cannon*

*I*t seems to me that a woman usually chooses the man who chooses her.

—*Emily Bennett*

*P*oor Kurt, I feel sorry for him. It was always, "I am Count von Haugwitz-Reventlow." He never forgot it—until one day I said, "Who cares? Who cares about the Count von Haugwitz-Reventlow today"—the world has come a long way from that sort of thing. A long way.

—*Barbara Hutton*

A man's home may be his castle on the outside, but it is his nursery inside.

—*Barbara Melton*

*T*he best decision I ever made in all my life was to marry my husband at the right time and in the right place.

—*Virginia Cook Sanders*

*I*f it please the king [my husband], and if I have found favour in his sight, and the thing seem right before the king, and I be pleasing in his eyes, let it be written to reverse the letters . . . to destroy the Jews which are in all the king's provinces:

For how can I endure to see the evil that shall come unto my people? or how can I endure to see the destruction of my kindred?

—*Esther*

*M*y Nade was the kindest gentleman I ever met. He was always a gentleman even around his horses.

—*Emma Riggs McKay*

*A*nd then . . . after all and all—when the prophet speaks the debate is over.

—*Elaine Cannon*

Gallimaufry

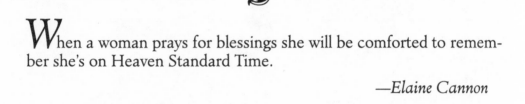

When a woman prays for blessings she will be comforted to remember she's on Heaven Standard Time.

—*Elaine Cannon*

We as a society abhor the taking of life, yet we give so little dignity to the method of its creation.

—*Anne Carroll Darger*

What we need in our nation is more conscience with our competence.

—*Lenore Lafount Romney*

*T*o everything there is a season, and a time to every purpose under the heavens. . . . That goes for ideas, too. If an idea doesn't work now, try it later. If an idea has seen its day, forget it and move on.

—*Bertha Reeder*

*T*here will always be people in the way—say "excuse me" and move on!

—*Lottie McKay*

*I*t takes great passion and energy to do anything creative. . . . You have to care so much that you can't sleep, you can't eat, you can't talk to people. It's just got to be right. You can't do it without that passion.

—*Agnes DeMille*

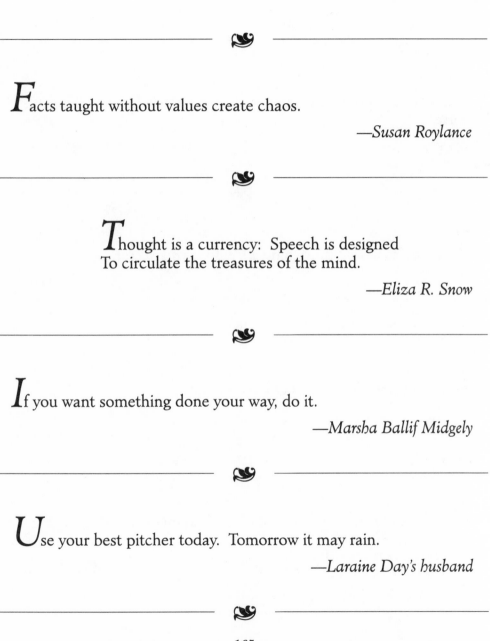

*F*acts taught without values create chaos.

—*Susan Roylance*

*T*hought is a currency: Speech is designed
To circulate the treasures of the mind.

—*Eliza R. Snow*

*I*f you want something done your way, do it.

—*Marsha Ballif Midgely*

*U*se your best pitcher today. Tomorrow it may rain.

—*Laraine Day's husband*

*A*lways keep your spurs on; you never know when you'll meet a horse.

—*Maureen Malaskey's mother*

*T*hink twice before burdening a friend with a secret.

—*Marlene Dietrich*

*I*f dreams never come true, stop dreaming.

—*Elizabeth Fuller*

*B*eware of fishing for compliments—you might come up with a boot.

—*Carol Weston*

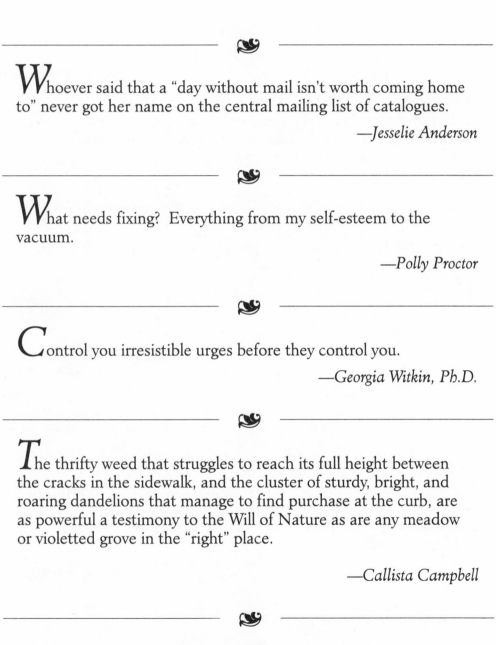

Whoever said that a "day without mail isn't worth coming home to" never got her name on the central mailing list of catalogues.

—*Jesselie Anderson*

What needs fixing? Everything from my self-esteem to the vacuum.

—*Polly Proctor*

Control you irresistible urges before they control you.

—*Georgia Witkin, Ph.D.*

The thrifty weed that struggles to reach its full height between the cracks in the sidewalk, and the cluster of sturdy, bright, and roaring dandelions that manage to find purchase at the curb, are as powerful a testimony to the Will of Nature as are any meadow or violetted grove in the "right" place.

—*Callista Campbell*

*T*he ideal necklace, the most universally becoming piece of jewelry ever created . . . is a string of pearls. Every woman should own a single strand pearl necklace, and a second one of three or five strands. . . . Like roses in a vase, an odd number is more elegant than an even on.

—*Genevieve Antoine Dariaux*

*P*hysical pain, however great, ends in itself and falls away like dry husks from the mind, whilst moral discords and nervous horrors sear the soul.

—*Alice James*

*I*n Russia, as I sat there day after day wearing headphones, listening to the interpreter struggle to make our words relevant, I wondered if we could establish meaningful rapport with a nation that had never seen raisins dance in dark glasses on TV . . . never had a garage sale.

—*Erma Bombeck*

---

*Y*a hafta earn what ya get!

—*Orphan Annie*

---

*L*ife comes one to a customer.

—*Elaine Cannon*

---

*T*hroughout the years I have set up my own rules about eating food: Never eat anything you can't pronounce. Beware of food that is described as, "Some Americans say it tastes like chicken."

—*Erma Bombeck*

---

*U*gly uglies are the other side of life. As you live you may see things you never want to see again. You may hear words that you wish you hadn't. Don't dwell on them. Remember, all life isn't like that and everybody is not involved in the ugly uglies. You aren't— by choice.

—*Elaine Cannon*

Spiritual maturity is understanding that we cannot blame anybody else for our problems.

—*Elaine Cannon*

Have you pondered lately what is said in James 3:2 about offending not in word? . . . The teaching goes on to suggest such a person is perfect and "able also to bridle the whole body." I like that. I am offended by obscene language, and I find it particularly offensive when a young woman or her mother succumb to using X-rated words.

—*Kiki Knickerbocker*

We are familiar with the traditional cultural imbalance between work and love, where women have been allowed authority only in the sphere of love while men attend to the work of the world. Such an imbalance results in a warped expression of the individual potential energy. For women: self-pity, masochism, manipulation, celebration of the torments of the heart, invalidism, madness. For men: slavery, war, corporate profits, destruction of the earth.

—*From Diaries of Women Vintage*

I must call for [the beer] industry's voluntary elimination of the types of alcohol advertising that appeal to youth on the basis of certain types of life-style appeals—sexual appeal, sports appeal, or risky activities.

—*Antonia Novella, U.S. Surgeon General*

*T*o everything there is a season. . . . Yes, a season to be young and doing the inimitable things of youth and a time to be relishing in the richness and understanding that maturity brings. But some people's timing is off. They marry when they're supposed to be having fun and have "fun" when they're supposed to be married. . . . They learn to cook after they're married and study the scriptures when they arrive in the mission field . . . or learn to behave properly after they've been embarrassed in a social situation . . . or value gospel principles after they've suffered the pangs of repentance. Personal timing should be clocked because there *is a time to every purpose under the heaven.*

—*Elaine Cannon*

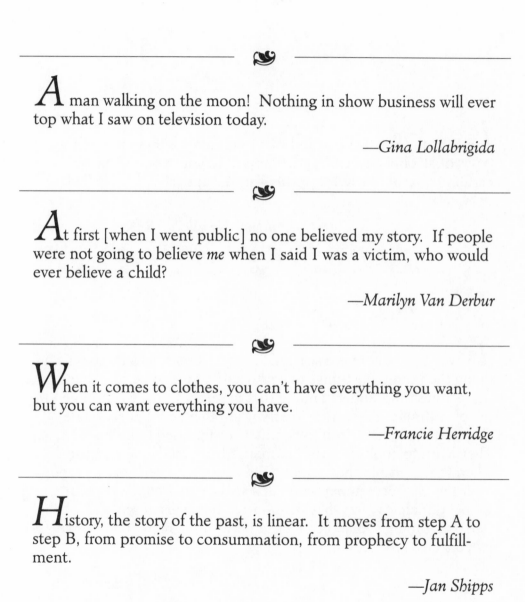

A man walking on the moon! Nothing in show business will ever top what I saw on television today.

—*Gina Lollabrigida*

*A*t first [when I went public] no one believed my story. If people were not going to believe *me* when I said I was a victim, who would ever believe a child?

—*Marilyn Van Derbur*

*W*hen it comes to clothes, you can't have everything you want, but you can want everything you have.

—*Francie Herridge*

*H*istory, the story of the past, is linear. It moves from step A to step B, from promise to consummation, from prophecy to fulfillment.

—*Jan Shipps*

You need to be free and clear to do. . . . Climbing the ladder of success depends on how quickly you can react, how quickly you can assess a situation, how quickly you can come to a conclusion . . . and to do whatever you have to do. I will stuff envelopes if that's what it means to get a job done.

—*Cheryl Boone Isaacs*

Computers are a great help in the office—there still are a lot of mistakes, but now they're nobody's fault.

—*Carla Cannon*

In an international conference on women's needs we were discussing abortion and sexually transmitted disease. Futile talk. Foolish solutions suggested. I dared to say, "What about teaching chastity?" I was being translated in five languages and confusion erupted. "What is chastity?"—and no one had an answer, and they didn't want to hear mine.

—*Elaine Cannon*

*M*ost of the world's needs are either so trivial they escape our notice—or so immense they defy our solution.

—*Julie Auchstetter*

*E*very sunset, every winter sky, every new-born anything, every burst of apple blossoms among new green leaves, every moment of joy reflected upon or remembered is singular evidence of the wonder of all of life.

—*Minnie Egan Anderson*

*T*he great ones have had much to say about honor. Reciting a pledge, expressing a creed, making a promise with the phrase "on my honor" or "I covenant" or "I promise" is lofty business. But saying so doesn't make it so. Doing does.

—*Elaine Cannon*

I still believe people are basically good at heart.

—*Anne Frank*

*D*eliver me from writers (artists, actors) who say the way they live doesn't matter. I'm not sure a bad person can write a good book. If art doesn't make us better, then what on earth is it for?

—*Alice Walker*

           *G*ive me your tired, your poor,
Your huddled masses yearning to breathe free,
The wretched refuse of your teeming shore,
Send these, the homeless, tempest-tost to me,
I lift my lamp beside the golden door.

—*Emma Lazarus*

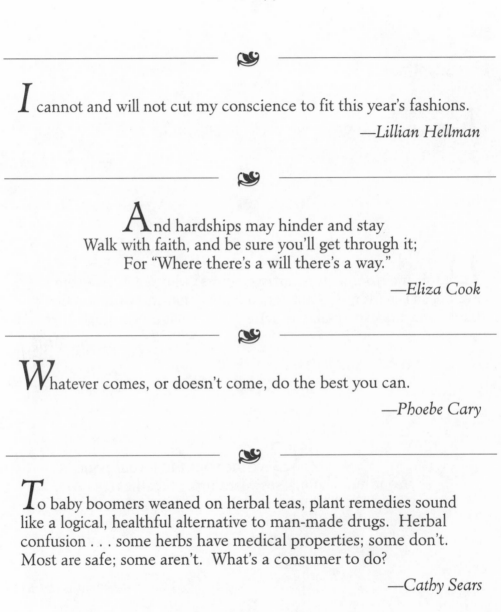

I cannot and will not cut my conscience to fit this year's fashions.

—*Lillian Hellman*

*A*nd hardships may hinder and stay
Walk with faith, and be sure you'll get through it;
For "Where there's a will there's a way."

—*Eliza Cook*

*W*hatever comes, or doesn't come, do the best you can.

—*Phoebe Cary*

*T*o baby boomers weaned on herbal teas, plant remedies sound
like a logical, healthful alternative to man-made drugs. Herbal
confusion . . . some herbs have medical properties; some don't.
Most are safe; some aren't. What's a consumer to do?

—*Cathy Sears*

———— 🦢 ————

*I*t's smart to be a Latter-day Saint.

—*LaRue Longden*

———— 🦢 ————

*W*hen you look like your passport photo, it's time to go home.

—*Erma Bombeck*

———— 🦢 ————

*S*he has hardening of the categories.

—*Janet Palmer*

———— 🦢 ————

*I*n hard times, if you can't eat it don't buy it!

—*Ruth Pingree Smith*

———— 🦢 ————

*B*eautiful faces are those that wear—
It matters little if dark or fair—
Whole-souled honesty printed there.

—*Ellen P. Allerton*

*T*he little cares that fretted me,
   I lost them yesterday
Among the fields above the sea, . . .

Among the singing birds,
   The humming of the bees.

—*Louise Imogen Guiney*

*T*here is no humorist like history.

—*Ariel Durant*

*B*uild for yourself a strong box,
    Fashion each part with care;
When it's strong as your hand can make it,
    Put all your troubles there;
Hide there all thought of your failures,
    And each bitter cup that you quaff;
Lock all your heartaches within it,
    Then sit on the lid and laugh.

                    —Bertha Adams Backus

*T*he fear of capitalism has compelled socialism to widen freedom, and the fear of socialism has compelled capitalism to increase equality. East is West and West is East, and soon the twain will meet.

                    —Ariel Durant

*T*he excursion is the same when you go looking for your sorrow as when you go looking for your joy.

                    —Eudora Welty

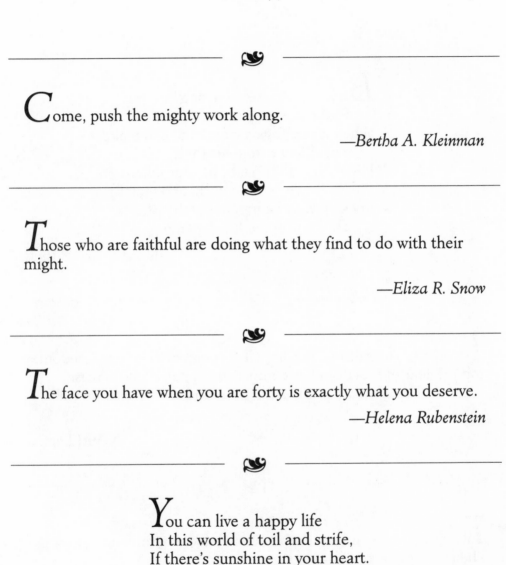

Come, push the mighty work along.

—*Bertha A. Kleinman*

Those who are faithful are doing what they find to do with their might.

—*Eliza R. Snow*

The face you have when you are forty is exactly what you deserve.

—*Helena Rubenstein*

You can live a happy life
In this world of toil and strife,
If there's sunshine in your heart.

—*Helen Silcott Dungan*

*S*atan isn't going to fuss much with the poor souls who have given in already.

—*Elaine Cannon*

*W*e shouldn't leave blanks in the story of our life. Dishonesty or attempts to cover up is the one thing that will invalidate [personal history].

—*Maureen Ursenbach Beecher*

*W*e are surrounded by people who "have it all" and yet have nothing—no joy. And there are just as many who have nothing, yet live in joy.

—*Laurel Bailey*

Why fear to-morrow, timid heart? . . .
We only need to do our part. . . .
And it will make our earth his heaven.

—*Lydia Avery Coonley Ward*

We give to the world peace or discomfort by what we speak. Our language and our conversations reveal our inner soul. No vulgar thoughts, no obscene words, but only say that which God can hear.

—*Virginia Weilenmann Anderson*

Out of the earth, the rose,
Out of the night, the dawn:
Out of my heart, with all its woes,
High courage to press on.

—*Laura Lee Mitchell*

*W*hen was yesterday?

—*Elizabeth Haglund*

*L*iterary study is strict discipline and hard work. . . . Let's not forget that it may also be joy.

—*Janet Palmer*

Golden Age

---

*S*ome people grow old but they never grow up.

—*Elaine Cannon*

---

*H*ow pleasant it is that always there's somebody older than you.

—*Florence Smith*

---

*Y*ou are never too young to fall in love and never too old to wish you had.

—*Carrie Noble*

---

*B*ackward, turn backward, O time, in your flight,
Make me a child again just for to-night!
Mother, come back from the echoless shore,
Take me again to your heart as of yore.

—*Elizabeth Akers Allen*

*M*y work at the Deseret Gym puts me in touch with a lot of hopeful women. One asked me about the secret for eternal youth, and I told her to grow up! Looking good when you are old enough to know about life is the best goal.

—*Evelyn Allen*

*L*ife is too short to have hurt feelings.

—*Florence Lane*

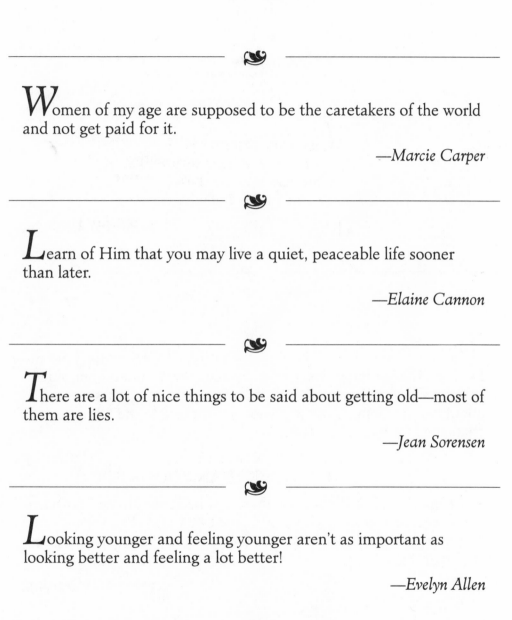

*W*omen of my age are supposed to be the caretakers of the world and not get paid for it.

—*Marcie Carper*

*L*earn of Him that you may live a quiet, peaceable life sooner than later.

—*Elaine Cannon*

*T*here are a lot of nice things to be said about getting old—most of them are lies.

—*Jean Sorensen*

*L*ooking younger and feeling younger aren't as important as looking better and feeling a lot better!

—*Evelyn Allen*

I have no Yesterdays.
   Time took them away;
Tomorrow may not be—
But I have Today!

—*Pearl Y. McGinnis*

*T*his afternoon I was a guest in a beautiful Chinese home here in Peking. The garden was enclosed by a high wall, and on one side, surrounded by twining red and white flowers, was a brass plate about two feet long. I asked someone to translate the Chinese characters for me. They said:

ENJOY YOURSELF
IT IS LATER THAN YOU THINK

I began to think about if for myself. I had not wanted another baby because I was still grieving for the one I lost. But I decided that moment that I should not wait any longer. Perhaps it may be later than I think, too.

—*Marguerite*

I've reached the stage where life seems so tenuous that I don't even buy green bananas.

—*Rosebud Marshall Jacobsen*

*I*t may be helpful to escape to memories when life gets depressing and stressful. But using memories as a standard for happiness today is immature.

—*Ardis Whitman*

*I*n all the wars women have grieved, "We'll never laugh again." I've lived through enough wars to know that we *do* laugh again— we'll just never be young again or truly innocent.

—*Minnie Egan Anderson*

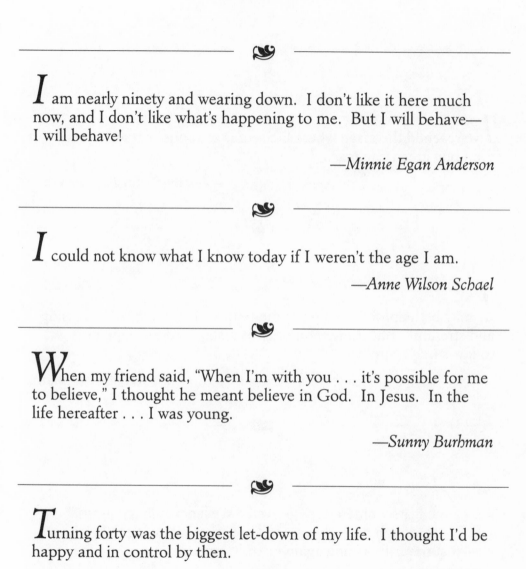

I am nearly ninety and wearing down. I don't like it here much now, and I don't like what's happening to me. But I will behave— I will behave!

—*Minnie Egan Anderson*

I could not know what I know today if I weren't the age I am.

—*Anne Wilson Schael*

*W*hen my friend said, "When I'm with you . . . it's possible for me to believe," I thought he meant believe in God. In Jesus. In the life hereafter . . . I was young.

—*Sunny Burhman*

*T*urning forty was the biggest let-down of my life. I thought I'd be happy and in control by then.

—*Janet Palmer*

Why . . . it's a mere trifle.

—*Mary Young Burton*

The good old days? . . . High school the best years of your life?
Well, I've heard the same thing about college, your twenties . . .
right up through retirement. . . . Every stage of life . . . will have its
moments—both good and bad. The best any of us can do is try to
get through the bad . . . and live for the good!

—*Cathi Hanauer*

Good Grief

We are here on earth to be proven, here on earth to endure—even flourish—until we are safely dead.

—*Elaine Cannon*

*T*here was a sorrow in my heart until I heard the flute of the wind whistling the grasses of the meadow, silencing the raven of doom, and this gentle whispering made my soul tranquil.

—*Abigail Jacobsen*

*O*ur very suffering and afflictions may be steps bringing us nearer to heaven.

—*Lillian Eichler Watson*

I reason, earth is short,
And anguish absolute.
And many hurt;
But what of that?

I reason, we could die:
The best vitality
Cannot excel decay;
But what of that?

I reason that in heaven
Somehow, it will be even,
Some new equation, given
But what of that?

—Emily Dickinson

I don't know about your children, but my offspring understand heaven to be furnished with fast food stalls dispensing glazed donuts and chocolate milk. Plus, they get a different mom.

—Elaine Cannon

Where I consider Life and its few years—
A wisp of fog betwixt us and the sun;
A call to battle, and the battle done . . .
I wonder at the idleness of tears.

Ye old, old dead, and ye of yesternight,
Chieftains, and bards, and keepers of the sheep,
By every cup of sorrow that you had,
Loose me from tears, and make me see alright
How each hath back what once he stayed to weep:
Homer his sight, David his little lad!

—Lizette Woodworth Reese

Though my soul may set in darkness, it will rise
    in perfect light,
I have loved the stars too fondly to be fearful
    of the night.

—Sarah Williams

*I*f we don't protect the most vulnerable in our society, from the very youngest to the very oldest, then which segment of our society will next be considered expendable?

—*Susan Thorne*

I didn't originate this idea but I believe it enough to repeat it. The saddest truth twixt now and then is thinking of what might have been.

—*Elaine Cannon*

I longed to see my husband who was dead. Why can we not call them to us in our grief and sorrow, why cannot our dead come back to us if only for one sweet hour.

—*Emmeline B. Wells*

I wish there were some wonderful place called the Land of Beginning Again, where all our mistakes and all our poor selfish grief could be dropped like a shabby old coat at the door, and never be put on again.

—*Louisa Fletcher*

*T*he first Christmases after a divorce, or any loss . . . are thin ice. Joy turns poignant on you; memory curdles; the things you have managed to keep the same only remind you of the things you have not.

—*Amanda Lovell*

*T*hough we all know that we must die,
Yet you and I
May walk like gods and be
Even now at home in immortality.

—*Louise Driscoll*

*I*t is one of life's tragedies when a person misplaces or discounts her soul—that forever part of us regardless of what happens to the body. The soul needn't be crippled just because the body happens to be.

—*Becky Reeve*

I will not grieve for what they have lost, I will rejoice in what they have gained.

I will not blame you for what happened; but I will thank you for what is happening now. To them, as they know you in person, to me, as I know you in spirit.

—*Marjorie Holmes*

I wish that the slow years would hurry! When, when will they bring all I dream of to me?

—*Margaret Johnson*

---

*T*hou dost not weep alone. . . . Hope eternal brings relief.

—*Eliza R. Snow*

---

*I*n keeping friends who grieve, simple gestures can bring comfort. But don't look for the silver lining. Efforts to minimize tragedy are not only ineffective, they deposit a truckload of guilt on the person who is suffering.

—*Lois Duncan*

I'd like my heaven afore I die."

—*Mary Webb*

---

*T*he difficulty about all this dying is that you can't tell a fellow anything about it, so where does the pen come in?

—*Alice James*

---

*W*hat profit is there finally, I said to myself, in all this round of never ceasing labor? Weaving cloth to buy dresses to wear out in weaving more cloth to buy more dresses. When my day is past, my warp and woof of life and labors ended and my body has gone to rest in the grave, What is there to mark the ground on which I trod? Nothing, and the thought made me weep.

—*Martha Cragun Cox*

I believe in the immortality of the soul because I have within me immortal longings.

—*Helen Keller*

*I*n my work and walks I've witnessed among people an increased belief in life after death—that immortality is no longer just a hope, it is a real possibility.

—*Elaine Cannon*

*T*he bustle in a house
The morning after death
Is solemnest of industries
Enacted upon earth,—

The sweeping up the heart,
And putting love away
We shall not want to use again
Until eternity.

—*Emily Dickinson*

*L*et us all watch over each other, that we may sit down in heaven together.

—*Eliza R. Snow*

*T*he whole world is mourning the loss of a prophet, but I have lost my husband.

—*Freda Joan Lee*

Generally people believe in life after death. They just don't know what to do about it.

—*Elaine Cannon*

I will control myself,
Or go inside.
I will not flaw perfection with my grief.
Handsome, this day:
No matter who has died.

—*Edna St. Vincent Millay*

*B*lessed are they who understand
My faltering step and palsied hand . . .
Blessed are they who never say,
You've told that story twice today . . .
Blessed are they who know I'm at loss
To find the strength to carry the cross.
Blessed are they who ease the day
Of my journey home in loving ways.

—*Esther May Walker*

*M*y heart is a honeycomb: Aching, wringing, wrenching, tenderness forced into memory by circumstance. Loving relationships canceled at the bier. Insistent pain and discarded dreams each in turn sealed off, walled up, capsulized against unbearable suffering.

—*Elaine Cannon*

*S*omeone asked me at a funeral why I was so weepy—if the deceased were a special loved one. I explained that I am just a weepy person—I even cry at the opening of a mall.

—*Evelyn Bennett*

*B*low through me, Life, pared down at last to bone,
So fragile and so fearless have I grown.

—*Anne Morrow Lindbergh*

I've tasted every victual and danced every dance; now there's one last tart I haven't bit on, one tune I haven't whistled. But I'm not afraid. I'm truly curious. Death won't get a crumb by my mouth I won't keep and savor. So don't you worry over me. Now, all of you go, and let me find my sleep.

—*Grandma Spaulding*

*O*ne day I'll close my eye, all unafraid,
And dear ones here will say, "The journey's end!"
That hour I shall find thee, undismayed;
God grant that I may thank thee, O my friend!

—*Blanche Kendall McKey*

*I*t's all right. Like everything else in this life, it [death] is fitting.

—*Great-grandma Spaulding*

*L*ord, I present myself before thee clean and pure. . . . Oh, and this is my beloved daughter Sharon.

—*LaRue Longden's last words*

*I*ntreat me not to leave thee, or to return from following after thee: for whither thou goest, I will go; and where thou lodgest, I will lodge: thy people shall be my people, and thy God my God:
    Where thou diest, will I die, and there will I be buried.

—*Ruth*

*S*peak thou, availing Christ!—and fill this pause.

—*Elizabeth Barrett Browning*

*T*hus through the troubled twilight of today
Emmaus road has stretched its shining thread.
And still Christ walks beside [us] on the way,
To hold the light of hope, to break the bread.

—*Ida Norton Munson*

*A*t a friend's funeral someone read the details of her will recorded in joy by her mother. At the end of her life here was proof and perspective about the beginning . . . at this dying, a kind of resurrection.

—*Elaine Cannon*

About the Compiler

A popular lecturer and author, Elaine Cannon is a graduate of the University of Utah and former general president of the Young Women.

Besides a long career in editing Church publications, she was for many years a regular contributor to national magazines, including *Better Homes and Gardens, Seventeen,* and other periodicals. She has received national awards for her writing and is the author or coauthor of numerous books, several of which have been translated into foreign languages. She has recorded many of her works and these are available on cassette tape.

For thirty years Elaine Cannon was a daily columnist for intermountain newspapers. She has hosted her own TV show and for several years was a featured speaker on a weekly radio program broadcast internationally.

She is married to D. James Cannon. They are the parents of six children.